WILLIAM ROBERT GROVE

THE LAWYER WHO INVENTED THE FUEL CELL

John Wilson
William Wilson
James M. Wilson

For Julian —

with kind thanks for helping at
the launch of this book, and very
best wishes for all of your writing
– looking forward to your book –
love Cecilly.

and all good wishes from us both.
John and Shirley.

WILLIAM ROBERT GROVE

THE LAWYER WHO INVENTED THE FUEL CELL

With Grove's 1888 Discourse on Antagonism

John Wilson
William Wilson
James M. Wilson

Metolius Ltd 2007

Published by Metolius Ltd, United Kingdom

Copyright © Metolius Ltd

Biography of William Robert Grove, scientist, lawyer, inventor of the fuel cell.

ISBN 0955 719 305   ISBN 978-0-9557193-0-1

For Edward, Sam, Alistair, David, Julian, Alex, Emma,
Shirley, Jane, Juliet, Jeffrey and Juliette

This account of the achievements of
a constructive and gifted Welshman

JW
WW
JW

Preface

For those working on the development of fuel cell technologies, the name of William Robert Grove is still remembered as the original inventor of the fuel cell in 1845. Every two years in London the Grove Fuel Cell Symposium brings together many hundreds of participants and companies from around the world, with a presentation of the Grove medal and a Grove exhibition. But his is not yet a name with which the wider public is familiar, like those of Faraday or Darwin. Perhaps this is because it has been so many years since Grove's discoveries, and their real potential has not yet been realized. Only now that the pressure to replace fossil fuels is increasing day by day is it clear that fuel cells could achieve ever greater practical importance, as shown in the section of this book contributed by James M. Wilson on the development of fuel cell potential since Grove.

Although Grove's name is associated with a Fuel Cell Symposium, some aspects of his life may be unknown even to fuel cell specialists. Grove's scientific achievement, as an inventor, researcher, lecturer and writer about science, was matched by a parallel and later legal career in which he rose to the top of that profession as well, becoming a Queen's Counsel, leading patent lawyer and High Court judge. The variety of his education and interests is reflected in the fact that the man who invented the nitric acid 'Grove Battery' and later the fuel cell, and wrote *The Correlation of Physical Forces* also played an important part in the defence of the notorious William Palmer, the Rugeley Poisoner, one of the most celebrated criminal cases of its century, and was a participant in many of the leading patent cases of his time.

A proud Welshman, born and brought up in Swansea, and later to return there in 1848 as Vice President for the annual meeting of the British Association for the Advancement of Science, Grove's scientific and legal interests came together in areas such as the earliest development of photography, where he not only gave lectures on the science of the new means of making photographic images, but corresponded with many of its earliest pioneers like Fox Talbot, and gave some of them advice on patent law and litigation.

i

It is this variety of interests, and his ability to bridge two widely different disciplines and to succeed at both, that first drew us to look at Grove's life. We have tried in this short biography to present to scientists and non-scientists alike a picture of Grove himself, his personal life, and his work as one of the leading scientists of his day and one of its leading lawyers.

John Wilson   **William Wilson**   **James M. Wilson**

Acknowledgements

We must first acknowledge our debt to Dr M.L. Cooper's 1987 PhD thesis for the Open University, *William Robert Grove (1811-96), Gentleman of Science*. This comprehensive and scholarly account of Grove's life is essential reading for anyone interested in Grove, and we have drawn freely on it and had useful guidance on sources from the detailed notes in it. We are most grateful to Dr Cooper for allowing us to make use of this thesis.

Of great value also, and equally recommended for further reading, is Dr Ulf Bossel's book *The Birth of the Fuel Cell*, which contains a great deal about the close relationship between Grove and Christian Friedrich Schoenbein, and prints the many letters they exchanged in a lively and engaging correspondence. The book sets out in detail Dr Bossel's researches on the way in which Schoenbein is to be credited with discovery of the 'fuel cell effect', while Grove went on to develop the first working fuel cell. We are grateful to Dr Bossel for his permission to quote from some of this correspondence.

On Grove's legal work, apart from law reports of the various cases in which he was involved, the Notable British Trials Series volume on the *Trial of William Palmer*, originally edited by George H. Knott and revised by Eric R. Watson has been used as our principal source on the trial of the Rugeley Poisoner, a classic of its kind, with verbatim accounts of Grove in action in cross examination and of his contributions to the unsuccessful defence. We have taken the picture of Palmer from the same source.

We must also thank Professor Frank James of the Royal Institution of Great Britain for giving us permission on behalf of the Institution and as editor of Faraday's correspondence to quote letters in the published volumes of that correspondence.

Our thanks to the many librarians who have helped with our researches must include Guy Holborn and Jo Hutchings at Lincoln's Inn Library and Ann Egan and Judy McCallum at the Llandrindod Wells Library, who have tracked down books and papers with much determination.

For the section on the development of fuel cell potential since Grove, we are very grateful for assistance from the following –

Norman Bessette PhD, CTO & Senior VP of Engineering, Accumentrics Corporation;

Dr. Michael Brower, Principal AWS Truewind;

Leonard S. Discenza, President Design By Analysis, Inc.;

Mohammad Enayatollah PhD, Vice President, Advanced Technology Co-Founder of Protonex Technology Corporation;

Alan Ludwiszewski PhD, Director of Engineering of Lilliputian Systems, Inc.;

Thomas Ollila, Plug Power, Inc.;

Gary Simon, President and Chief Executive Officer, Accumentrics Corporation;

G. Bikley Stevens II, Managing Partner, Ardour Capital Investments, LLC;

James Rosenfield, Co-Founder Source2, Co-Founder Cambridge Energy Research Associates;

Dr Kerry-Ann Adamson, Manager, Fuel Cell Today.

We are grateful to Russ Ticehurst of Digitech Services Ltd for all the computer work in preparing this book for production.

We are most grateful to Juliet Evans for her expert proof-reading and sub-editing skills; and to Shirley Moran for reading and correcting the text.

Other books or sources which have provided valuable information include:

Sir Henry Lyons *The Royal Society 1660-1945* (Cambridge, 1944), whose account of Grove's role in the reform of the Royal Society we found invaluable.

J.G. Crowther *Statesmen of Science* (Cressell Press 1965), with a valuable section on Grove.

Francis Galton FRS *English Men of Science: Their Nature and Nurture* (1874).

Robin Lenman (Ed) *The Oxford Companion to the Photograph* (Oxford University Press, 2005), which contains valuable pen portraits of early photographers and useful background explanations of photographic techniques.

Smithsonian National Museum of American History - Bearing Center and their website Collecting History of Fuel Cells- A Smithsonian Research Project. http://americanhistory.si.edu/fuelcells/

Fuel Cell Today.com

Solid Oxide Fuel Cell Technology.
http://americanhistory.si.edu/fuelcells/so/sofemain.htm. (7/30/2007)

Fuel Cell Basics- Historical Perspective.
http://fctec.com/fctec_history.asp (8/01/2007)

http://www.fuelcelltoday.com/Fuelcelltoday.com/Educationcentre/Educ ationCentreExternal/Educationkit/html (7/18/07)

Fuel Cell Origins: 1880-1965.
htpp://americanhistory.si.edu/fuelcells/origins/origins2.html (8/14/2007)

Girvan, Ray, *"Fuel from the past"*, Scientific Computing World: Oct/Nov 2005. http//www.scientific-computing.com/features/features.php?feature_id=29 (8/1/07).

Fuel Cells the first 120 years. (7/18/07)

Phosphoric Acid Fuel Cells. http://americanhistory.si.edu/fuelcells/phos/pafeman.htm (7/31/2007).

PEM Fuels Cell Technology. http://american history.si.edu/fuelcells/pem/pemmani.htm (7/21/2007) Molten Carbonate Fuel Cell Technology. http://americanhistory.si.edu/fuelcells/mc/mcfemain.htm (7/31/2007)

Crawley, Gemma, Direct Methanol Fuel Cells (DMFC) http://www.fuelcelltoday.com/FuelCellToday/FCTFiles/FCTArticleFile s/Article_1194_DMFC%20Technology%20Article.pdf (8/1/2007).

"Huge Growth Potential of the Fuel Cells Market Due to Energy Efficiency and Environmental Concerns", March 31,2007 http://thebusinessaddition.com/huge-growthpotential-for-the-fuel-cell-market-due-to-energy-efficiency-and-environmental-concerns-623/ (7/30/2007).

Page   **Contents**

Illustrations

Cover
Sir William Robert Grove, photograph in 1844 by David Octavius Hill and Robert Adamson, taken at the British Association for the Advancement of Science meeting at Nottingham in 1844
©Scottish National Portrait Gallery

Michael Faraday by Thomas Phillips
©National Portrait Gallery

Fuel cell sketch from Grove's letter to Faraday
22 October 1842, Letter 1441 Faraday's published correspondence,
©Professor Frank James, Royal Institution

Fuel cell drawing from Grove's December 1842 paper 'On a Gaseous Voltaic Battery' Philosophical Magazine

Grove's 1843 development of his fuel cell drawings
Philosophical Transactions 1843 – 'On the Gas Voltaic Battery – Experiments made with a view of ascertaining the rationale of its action and its application to Eudiometry'

Grove's 1845 drawings of the fuel cell apparatus
Philosophical Transactions 1845 – 'On the Gas Voltaic Battery – Voltaic Action of Phosphorous, Sulphur and Hydrocarbons'

Lithograph of Grove by W. Bosley, after a Daguerrotype by Antoine Claudet, 21 February 1849
©Bridgeman Art Library

Sir William Robert Grove by John Jabez Edwin Mayall,
London Daguerrotypist
©National Portrait Gallery

Cover of the 1856 Times Report of the Trial of William Palmer for poisoning John Parsons Cook, showing the Talbot Arms at Rugeley where Cook met his end

"The Accurst Surgeon" – **Grove's client, William Palmer, the Rugeley Poisoner** – from The Trial of William Palmer, ed. G.H. Knott, Eric R. Watson

"Drs Taylor and Rees performing their analysis" – from the 1856 Times Report of the Palmer Trial, a popular view of "sound science"

Sir William Robert Grove, as High Court Judge, by the London Stereoscopic & Photographic Company
©National Portrait Gallery

THE LAWYER WHO INVENTED THE FUEL CELL

Scientists today tend to specialise and to engage in deep research into relatively minute problems. It is difficult now to imagine someone from another profession playing an important part in scientific enquiry. Still less is it possible to imagine such an outsider inventing something that would ultimately prove to be of great importance.

Just over 160 years ago, however, a young Welsh barrister managed to pursue two callings, as an original research scientist and as a lawyer with a demanding practice at the bar. This man, William Robert Grove, was born in Swansea, a city that has often produced men with lively minds and unique talents – Dylan Thomas and Vaughan Williams were, in their day, together at Swansea Grammar School. Grove's father played an important part in Swansea's municipal life and was a magistrate and Deputy Lieutenant of Glamorgan. Grove's mother was a Bevan.

In 1873 a Fellow of the Royal Society, Francis Galton, a cousin of Charles Darwin and a strong believer in hereditary ability, sent a detailed questionnaire to his colleagues about their early interest in science, their family and educational background, religious and political affiliation and even "Temperament, if distinctly nervous, sanguine, bilious, or lymphatic", "measurement round inside of your hat" and "energy of mind, if remarkable". Half of them responded and he published the results in his *English Men of Science: Their Nature and Nurture* in 1874. One of the anonymous participants, later identified as William Grove, was recorded as saying, "My first start was reading a child's story called the "Ghost", where a philosophical elder brother cures his younger brother of superstition, by showing him experiments with phosphorus, electricity etc. This set me on making an electrical machine with an apothecary's phial etc. I was then about 12 years old. My grandfather had scientific tastes to some degree. My grandfather's brother...was a good amateur chemist and astronomer..." (Grove, incidentally, said that the circumference of his head was 24 inches). He later said "it was from my grandfather that I received my first notions of physical science. I can recollect, when not more than seven or eight years old, hearing from him an explanation of why three planets above the horizon at the same time would be always nearly in a straight line, they being necessarily in the plane of the elliptic."

Young Grove did not go to school but was educated at home by tutors. When he went on to Brasenose College at Oxford he studied classics, apparently without enthusiasm, showing no sign of his later energy and enquiring mind. He ended up in 1829 with a mere pass degree. He went on to study law at Lincoln's Inn and was called to the bar in 1835.

But he soon showed a pronounced interest in science (then known as "natural philosophy") particularly in engineering and electricity. In that same year, 1835, at the age of 24, he joined the Royal Institution and became a founder member of the Swansea Literary and Philosophical Society, later to become the Royal Institution of South Wales.

Two years later, still at Swansea, he married Emma Maria, daughter of John Diston Powles, a fellow member of the Royal Institution. They went on to have six children, though one daughter died in infancy and another drowned in Loch Awe at the age of 21. He found it a struggle to support a large family, especially as he himself described his health as "very indifferent, strong frame but weak & torpid liver" with kidney pains for which he took opium. But nevertheless he found time to work on methods of improving batteries, most of which at the time ran down very quickly.

The battery had been invented in Italy in 1800. Luigi Galvani had found that contact of two different metals with the muscle of a frog resulted in electric current. His friend Alessandro Volta, professor of physics at Como and later at Padua, experimented with metals and found that animal tissue was not needed to produce a current. He demonstrated the first electric battery, later called the voltaic pile or simply a voltaic cell, in 1800. He was honoured by Napoleon and the Emperor of Austria and the volt was later so named in his honour. Grove admired Volta. The word voltaic constantly recurs in his scientific disquisitions and he described the original fuel cell as a voltaic pile.

At the age of 28 he devised the first of his notable cells, the nitric acid battery, and described it at a meeting of the British Association for the

Advancement of Science. It consisted of zinc in dilute sulphuric acid and platinum in concentrated nitric acid, separated by a porous pot. This, the 'Grove Cell', was the favourite battery of the early American telegraph, offering a strong current output but it was found that it discharged poisonous nitric gas and large telegraph offices were filled with gas from rows of hissing Grove batteries. As telegraphs became more complex the need for constant voltage became critical and the Grove device was necessarily limited because as the cell discharged, nitric acid was depleted and voltage was reduced. Nevertheless the invention of this cell made a considerable impression, and led Grove to become well known in many parts of the world. Michael Faraday, the distinguished scientist and communicator whose expertise was mainly in the fields of electricity and magnetism, invited him to describe this battery at one of the Royal Institution's evening discourses. On this occasion Grove demonstrated the power of his battery, when it was used to short-circuit the terminals, by destroying the blade of Faraday's pocket knife. He was also able to tell his audience that his cell had been used by an electrical engineer to propel a boat on the river Neva at St. Petersburg, an early demonstration of electricity being used as a driving mechanism.

In the same year, 1840, the young lawyer was elected a Fellow of the Royal Society. The following year he was chosen to be Professor of Experimental Philosophy at the London Institution, which had been founded to bridge the gap between science and business. The need for this formed the theme of his inaugural lecture *"On the progress of physical science since the opening of the London Institution"*. He was a founder member of the Chemical Society in 1841.

In 1842, at the age of 31, he announced his invention of the gas battery, the origin of the fuel cell which, though neglected for many years, was to be brought out of obscurity in the 20th century and would provide power for the Gemini and Apollo space crafts and electricity and water for the space shuttle.

On the 22nd October of that year Grove wrote to Michael Faraday saying –

"My dear Sir,

I have just completed a curious voltaic pile which I think you would like to see, it is composed of alternate tubes of oxygen & hydrogen through each of which passes platina foil so as to dip into separate vessels of water acidulated with sulphuric acid the liquid just touching the extremities of the foil as in the rough figure below.

The platina is platinized so as to expose by capillary attraction a greater surface of liquid to the gas, with 60 of these alternations I get an unpleasant shock & decompose not only iodide of potassium but water so plainly that a continuous stream of fine bubbles ascends from each electrode. Thus water is decomposed by its composition – no oxidable metal is employed. I have reversed the tubes & tried all the counter expts but the phenomena are too marked I think to render any mistakes possible. Mr. Gassiot was with me today & saw the Expts. Can you spare me an hour next week on Tuesday if it suits you or any day except Wednesday at any hour from 11 – 3 – at the Laboratory of the London Institution. I cannot but regard the experiment as an important one both as to the chemical & other theories of the pile & as to the catalytic effect of the combination of the gases by platina.

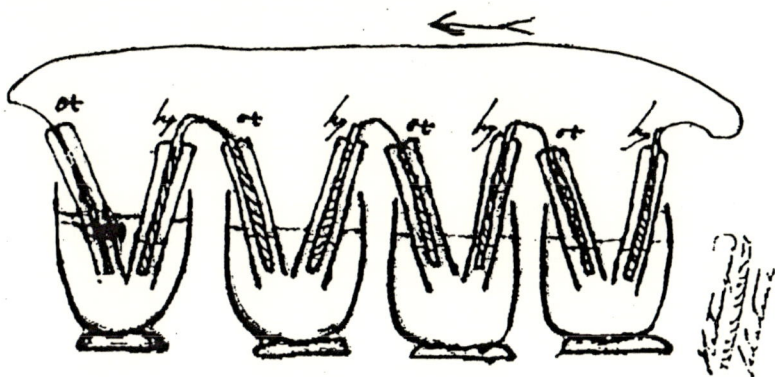

I remain my dear Sir yours very sincerely

W R Grove."

4

The original has been described as an electrochemical device which converted conventional fuel continuously into electricity. Sending an electric current through water splits the water into its component parts of hydrogen and oxygen. Grove reversed the reaction, combining hydrogen and oxygen to produce electricity and water. His practical solution built on the work of a Swiss professor, Christian Friedrich Schoenbein, who in 1838 discovered the fuel cell effect, while Grove converted theory into practice, so inventing what Ludwig Mond and Charles Langer were later to call the fuel cell. Schoenbein went on to discover ozone and to invent gun cotton. He and Grove became and remained good friends and corresponded regularly.

Grove's battery used zinc in dilute sulphuric acid and platinum in concentrated nitric acid. Curiously his gas battery, though it was to lead, ultimately, to the use of fuel cells in many applications today, and to more being projected, seems at the time to have aroused less interest than the earlier nitric acid battery. It is, however, Grove's chief claim to lasting fame.

The young barrister and research scientist was, at this stage of his life, possessed of remarkable energy. He lectured on all manner of topics – optics, galvanism, voltaic combinations, magnetism, "the physical elements of the ancient philosophers", the progress of science, light, electricity and solids, liquids and gases. From 1840 on he lectured 14 times to Friday evening meetings of the Royal Institution. These were attended by leading scientists but were mainly intended for a lay audience. It was not easy to present a serious account of scientific progress while making it intelligible to non-scientists. Grove however, seemed to be skilful at bridging the gap between the expert and the amateur. His lectures usually concluded with demonstrations of experiments which the audience found compulsive viewing. Twice he gave the Bakerian lecture at the Royal Society. He also wrote articles for *Blackwood's Magazine*.

In 1846, at the age of 35, he published the first edition of his magnum opus, *On the Correlation of Physical Forces*, on the interrelationship between the forces of 'Light, Heat, Electricity, Magnetism, Motion and Chemical Affinity'. In more speculative vein he asked rhetorically,

"Why is England a great nation? Is it because her sons are brave? No, for so are the savage denizens of Polynesia: She is great because their bravery is fortified by discipline, and discipline is the offshoot of science. Why is England a great nation? She is great because she excels in Agriculture, in Manufactures, in Commerce. What is Agriculture without Chemistry? What Manufactures without Mechanics? What Commerce without Navigation? What Navigation without Astronomy?"

The essay went through six editions, each containing new material. Some knowledgeable people were impressed by one or other edition of Grove's book. The Admiralty hydrographer said he was astonished at Grove's grasp of thought and depth of insight and considered the book as one of the most remarkable of the century. And, according to his niece Frances Wedgwood, Darwin went so far as to say that the idea of the correlation of force was one of far greater scope than that of evolution, or even the Newtonian theory of gravitation. But others took a different view. "Try to read Grove's book", wrote the Professor of Natural Philosophy at Edinburgh, "and tell me whether you feel all along the impression of humbug. I…cannot manage more than a few pages without falling asleep…" But by some Grove was given credit for first setting out the theory of force conversion. He himself wrote that "I believe myself to have been the first who introduced this subject as a generalised system of philosophy, and continued to enforce it in my lectures and writings for many years, during which it met with the opposition usual and proper to novel ideas." He did propound the principle of the conservation of energy a year before the German physicist Hermann von Helmholtz did so. And his book has recently been interpreted as offering "a model for the most efficient and economic means of organising a scientific community."

Almost by chance Grove now found a role that demanded both the trained mind of a lawyer and a knowledge of scientific progress and needs. For the newly elected FRS became one of the chief architects, indeed perhaps the chief architect, of the reform of the Royal Society to ensure that its scientific character should be strengthened and maintained. For two hundred years scientists had been in a minority in the Society, which had been dominated by wealthy non-scientists brought in after 1660 to keep it solvent. All this was about to change and Grove was one of those mainly responsible for the change.

At the age of 35 he was elected to the Society's Council. In 1846 he was made a member of the Charter Committee which planned the new reforms. He was one of those who advocated limiting the number of Fellows, and it was recorded that "Mr. Grove succeeded in his proposition for altering the then existing practice in the election of Fellows." Sir Henry Lyons FRS, in his book *The Royal Society 1660-1940*, wrote - "Very few Fellows of the Society have rendered to it such valuable services as did Sir William Grove. Sir Isaac Newton re-organised its Councils...Sir John Lubbock...improved and modernised the financial procedure of the Society...Sir William Grove, twenty years later, showed the Council how the proportion of non-scientific Fellows could be reduced and the scientific standard of the Society raised without any modification of the Charter..."

The successful reformers, led by Grove, set up a dining club called the "Philosophical Club" which was not merely a social club but, as Sir Henry Lyons records, was to "aim at checking any retrograde influences which might make their appearance in the policy of the Councils, stimulating the intellectual activity of the members and strengthening the influence of science in Great Britain." The club flourished for a good many years. In 1848 Grove was elected one of the Society's two Secretaries, so that in the first year after the revision of the statutes he could keep any eye on their implementation.

The battle for reform had been won, but it had been quite a bitter contest. The President, The Marquis of Northampton, and the Senior Secretary had both strongly opposed the reforms. Both resigned. The members of the Philosophical Club tried to get Grove elected as Senior Secretary, but he had perhaps wounded too many susceptibilities, and their efforts failed. Perhaps as something of a recompense he was awarded the Society's Royal Medal for his work on the gas battery.

The Librarian of the Royal Institution, K.D.C. Vernon, spoke in a Library Circle Meeting in 1966 of "the immense reputation which Grove had" adding, "He was at the very centre of scientific affairs in this country, and everybody – wealthy noblemen, famous scientists, and even an impecunious curate – wrote to him for his advice for his help and weighty support in matters of science. The curate, incidentally, wanted a free copy of *On the Correlation of Physical Forces* because he had six children and was too poor to buy it."

Vernon listed the large numbers of letters to Grove from distinguished scientists, now held by the Royal Institution, and besides saying he was a prominent figure in the history of the Institution said that Grove "was reputed to have a very bad temper" and that "he loved exercise and used to walk daily between the Law Courts and his home in Harley Street."

In 1846 Grove's membership of the Athenaeum Club was being considered under rule 2 which referred to the admission of persons "of distinguished eminence in Science, Literature, or the Arts, or for Public Services." Faraday had proposed Grove for membership in 1844 and when asked to provide proof that rule 2 was fulfilled, replied –

> "In answer to you enquiry respecting Mr. Grove I send you the following as the evidences of his philosophical character. First the battery called by his name which though it has not perhaps been formally described is known to every worker in Electricity: it puts into the space of 3 or 4 cubic feet that which at the Royal Institution employed the whole of a large room and because of its power, compactness economy and facility of use is the battery I use to the exclusion of almost every other.
>
> Next the Gas Voltaic battery, a very remarkable discovery & application in reference to the principles of voltaic action and which even promises useful practical results. After these come researches on the inactivity of amalgamated Zinc – on Electro Nitrurets – and on the Voltaic action of nonconductors such as Phosphorus Sulphur, & Hydrocarbons with other smaller things.
>
> He has published papers in the Philosophical Transactions of 1840, 1843 & 1845, & is at present on the Council of the Royal Society. He has also published many notices in the Comptes Rendus & the Philosophical Magazine."

Grove was duly elected, but not until 1851.

He was at this period at the pinnacle of his standing as a scientist, but practical considerations now became of overriding importance, so in the mid 1840s he finally concluded that he could no longer manage to pursue two careers. Although his real love was science, and he never lost his interest in all aspects of it, he found that he could not earn enough as a scientist to finance work on experiments and maintain a large family. He could earn much more as a barrister so he was determined to make that his main occupation. In January 1844, in a letter to Schoenbein, he wrote, "I have nearly made up my mind to give up my professorship on 25th of March next. I find like you that money is actually necessary & as I have now 4 children I must put my shoulder to the wheel. I do not intend altogether to give up science whatever leisure time I have I shall devote to it." Then, and subsequently, Schoenbein much regretted Grove's decision and strove to persuade him not to abandon science. "I am rather sorry, " he now wrote "for your giving up the professorship at the London Institution…for it was a means by which you were kept in close contact with science. Pray don't altogether abandon the latter…I trust….that your genius will not permit you to leave entirely the paths of science and drown yourself in the turbid floods of law."

Grove took his time. But in 1846 he finally resigned the professorship, which had paid only a meagre salary. Thereafter he concentrated on his law practice, which prospered. He took silk in 1852 on the South Wales and Chester Circuits. He did consider briefly applying for the chair of chemistry at Oxford but decided against facing a contested election. In 1852 he still lectured at the Royal Society on "The electro-chemical polarity of gases". Faraday wrote of this, "Having carefully read Mr. Grove's paper I arrive at the conclusion that it is correct in the experiments and sound in the deductions and touching as it does upon the unity of electrical phenomena, whether in the static or dynamic form, is of great value in the development of that part of science. My voice therefore is for the paper. Personally I hail it as a great aid in the expansion of that subject which I love". Grove kept in touch with the Royal Institution for a number of years, but effectively his career as a research scientist was over. The twenty years from 1835 to 1855 had been full of intense activity but now, in his mid-forties, he settled down to a steady career at the Bar.

He lived a comfortable life and often stayed with friends in France. Writing to Schoenbein in October 1857 he said, "I am here with my family, enjoying the hospitality of my kind friend M. Sequin. There is much to interest here a large house built on the ruins of an old abbey with endless woods, fishing, shooting etc the chateau of Buffon which belongs to the Sequins' son in law close by & which is itself built on the walls of an old chateau of the Duke of Burgundy. The gardens are excessively beautiful & we have had some moonlight promenades there. Add to this a kind & excellent family with which & mine the most delightful relations exist & but one regret is left that we must quit it for the fog & worry of a London life..." He also had a busy social life at home. Notable people in different walks of life were guests at his dinner table. A letter which survives at the Royal Institution written in June 1854 says -

"My Dear Mrs. Grove,

If we were to pop in on Monday Evening about 7 or ½ p.7 oclk in hopes of finding dinner over & you, my friend Grove, and the children (bless them) with nothing to do other than bear with our company is there any chance of our finding such to be the case?

Ever Most truly Your faithful Servant

M. Faraday"

Grove enjoyed grouse shooting and trout fishing. But his scientific outlook never deserted him. Once, while fishing in France, he noted white patches developing on the body of a trout and judged that this must be due to the effect of sunlight on one part of the body and not on others. He checked this by experiment, covering part of the body of a fish with a leaf and leaving the rest exposed to the sun. This proved that his surmise was correct.

The whole family were full of enterprise. When he was 58 Grove, in another letter to Schoenbein, said that he could walk 20 miles a day without fatigue, adding, "My wife which is a little older than I am went this spring with her son & daughter to Naples as fast as they could to see the eruption on Vesuvius. My son who is as perhaps you know a great alpine climber having this year ascended the Matterhorn. He got on the plateau of Vesuvius by night when it was in full eruption & has published a very interesting account of it." In fact Grove's son was the first person to climb the Matterhorn from both the Italian and Swiss sides.

This elder son became President of the Alpine Club and author of "The Frosty Caucuses" and several plays. The younger son, Coleridge Grove, took a first in mathematics at Balliol and then went into the Army, becoming a Major General and earning a C.B.

Grove himself maintained an early interest in telescopes, addressing the Royal Astronomical Society in 1853 on ways of improving them.

In 1866 he was appointed President of the British Association for the Advancement of Science for its annual meeting held at Nottingham. This body sought to promote and invigorate science, to stimulate research and present science to the public. Grove was the first president of it to announce publicly his support for Darwin's theory of evolution by natural selection. His Presidential Address to a large mixed audience at the Theatre Royal in Nottingham was received with acclaim although it lasted for almost two hours. His theme was, he said, continuity, that knowledge was a continuous process reached by small steps. This he illustrated by a large number of examples from natural history. Inevitably this led to a discussion of evolution. It was only seven years since Darwin had published *The Origin of Species* with its doctrine of descent from a single ancestor, achieved by the survival of the fittest and consequent modification. There was still a bitter argument between those who supported the new doctrine of evolution and those who still clung to the previous near universal assumption that all species had been separately created and could not be changed. Inevitably Grove's cautious venture into this controversial territory was welcomed by fellow scientists but subjected him to some strong criticism from others. Darwin himself thought Grove's argument was good and

11

original, though he considered that Grove's discussion of species was so vague that no real opinion emerged. But Grove had touched a raw nerve with the creationists, those "who are content to say God willed it." He asked if it would "not be more reverent and more philosophical to inquire by observation and experiment as to the probabilities of such frequent miraculous interventions?" There were inevitably some violent reactions to what were described as the seeds of infidelity and atheism. One leader writer said that "continuity is to be the new cant scientific term for the origin of everything."

It is sad that Grove's need to make a speech at the Mayor's banquet for 200 made him over an hour late in arriving to speak at a meeting of working men, who had asked for an address and were understandably indignant at being kept waiting so long and then being fobbed off with a brief and scrappy talk. This was a sad error of judgement on Grove's part.

At this Northampton meeting, however, Grove persuaded the Association to hold their 1867 annual meeting in Swansea, and took a leading part in organising the program there. It was not altogether easy as at that date the railway running west only reached Bristol and to get on to Swansea you had to take a coach overland or a boat round the coast. For Grove it was a moving experience to bring the leading scientists of the day to the city where he had been born and brought up, and he only wished that his father could have lived to see it.

Grove himself lived to be 86 but in the last 25 years of his life he was no longer much involved in science, though in 1872 he gave evidence to the Devonshire Commission on the need for scientific instruction and the advancement of science. Instead, in his sixties and seventies, he progressed from the bar to the bench and was recognised as a distinguished legal figure. At the age of 61 he was appointed a judge to the Court of Common Pleas. Next year he was knighted and at the age of 65, following the consolidation of the courts, he became a Judge of the High Court. His wife died in 1879 and next year he was appointed a Judge of the Queen's Bench. He was well regarded as a judge, but retired from the bench in 1887 and was sworn of the Privy Council. He returned to scientific studies but did no more original research. In the 1890s he suffered a long illness culminating in his death in 1896.

In an anonymous article which he wrote for *Blackwood's Magazine* in 1843 Grove contrasted the legacies of Alexander, whose empire fell apart almost as soon as he died, and Archimedes, whose invention left us with "the lever, the pulley, the mirror..." and if he returned he would trace the influence of his mind "in the power-loom, the steam-engine, in the building of the Royal Exchange, in the Great Britain steamship.." He also compared the achievement of Napoleon, who "applied the energies of a sagacious and comprehensive intelligence to his own policy of aggrandizement" and was the cause of sacrificing the lives of two million, with James Watt, with more modest talents – "Walk ten miles in any manufacturing district, enter any coal-mine, examine the Bank of England, travel by the Great Western railway, or navigate the Danube, the Mediterranean, the Indian or the Atlantic Ocean – in each and all of these that giant slave, the steam engine, will be seen..."

It is indeed true that there are two types of notable people – the destructive and the constructive. Grove himself led an eminently constructive life, applying a young and vigorous mind to invention and then to the organisation of science in the United Kingdom, while he had a happy family life and achieved distinction in the legal world.

In his response to Francis Galton's questionnaire he said of himself, according to Galton's notes: "business habits bad except what is the result of long discipline, but always punctual in appointments. Great want of curiosity as to the ordinary subjects of human gossip, but great love of solving scientific mysteries. Little interest in science as soon as it becomes exact and reducible to number and weight but great interest in solving enigmas such as chemical and electrical phenomena..."

He was not in fact much interested in the practical application of scientific discoveries. In an address to the Chemical Society he described his outlook in a nutshell: "For my own part, I must say that science to me generally ceases to be interesting as it becomes useful." Explaining this remarkable proposition, he continued, "Englishmen have a great liking for the practical power of science. I like it as a means of extending our knowledge beyond its ordinary grasps, leading us to know more of the mysteries of the universe."

Addressing young doctors at St. Mary's Hospital in May, 1869 Grove concluded by saying, "After delivering prizes…I may be expected to end with the usual encouraging peroration, that industry and ability command success; but I cannot, except in a modified form, agree to this copy-book maxim…The road to success is often that which a high-minded man cannot travel; he cannot learn to fetch and carry, to subserve the interest of a patron or a mob…I would fain endeavour to inculcate upon my younger hearers a higher motive than the mere hope of fame, wealth or power. If these come by an unswerving career, make good use of them; if not, console yourselves with the conviction that those who are said to be in power are frequently the veriest slaves in existence; that the improvement of our race is more promoted by those who think than by those who act…silent, proud, unappreciated martyrdom is commonly the lot of those whose labour tends most to advance mankind for upon them rests the burden of opposing existing prejudices and unsettling vested interests. Have courage to risk this. Your most noble profession offers the grandest field for human exertion – the widest scope for progressive improvement. To assuage human anguish…to convert despair into hope…will be often your lot…Meet failure without repining and success without exulting…."

Grove is still a great name for those who work in the world of fuel cells, but not widely known outside it. Increasing use of fuel cells in space technology, terrestrial transportation, industry, electricity generation, submarine propulsion and combined heat and power ought to ensure that his name becomes much more widely known, despite the century and a half between his discoveries and their full application.

In 2007 the President of Honda, Tukeo Fukui, was reported to have said that he believed the hydrogen fuel cell engine would one day sweep the world's car markets. "Hybrid cars alone cannot deal with global warming. The ultimate solution is the fuel cell but our engineers are struggling with this technical challenge and a breakthrough is not going to be easy," he said " at the moment it uses a massive amount of precious metal (platinum) and I don't think it's realistic for the next 10 years." Mr. Fukui said the technology would not be viable until consumers could re-supply the fuel cells at home from solar batteries that are carbon neutral.

All this suggests that we should seek to know more about the man who started the process by making the first fuel cell.

GROVE, SCHOENBEIN AND THE ORIGINS OF THE FUEL CELL

THE GAS VOLTAIC 'GROVE' BATTERY

Both Antoine-Cesar Becquerel and J.F. Daniell had worked on the problem of improving the functioning of zinc-copper cells or very early batteries. In 1829 Becquerel started to use two liquids separated by a porous partition, in order to overcome polarisation, and J.F. Daniell developed this further by separating copper sulphate solution from sulphuric acid by a partition made of unglazed earthenware.

Grove in turn experimented with different combinations of metals and electrolytes, before announcing that his preferred combination was of zinc in dilute sulphuric acid and platinum in concentrated nitric acid (or a mixture of nitric and sulphuric acid) . As we have seen, this Grove battery proved to be effective, but led Daniell to enter into a scrappy and sometimes rather ill tempered correspondence in 1842 in the Philosophical Magazine, implying (which Grove denied) that Grove must have drawn on his own ideas in order to invent his 'Grove' battery, while he Daniell apparently owed no similar debt to Becquerel.

GROVE, SCHOENBEIN AND THE FUEL CELL

Dr Ulf Bossel in his book *The Birth of the Fuel Cell 1835-1845* notes that Christian Friedrich Schoenbein had observed and discovered what he calls the "fuel cell effect" when writing an article *On the Voltaic Polarization of certain Solid and Fluid Substances* in the January 1839 issue of the *Philosophical Magazine* that …"we are entitled to assert that the current in question is caused by the combination of hydrogen with (the) oxygen (contained in dissolved water) and not by contact…" When he visited England in 1839, Schoenbein met Faraday, and carried out some of his polarization experiments there.

Schoenbein had been born in 1799 in Swabia, but was obliged to leave school at the age of fourteen, when he became an apprentice in a chemical and pharmaceutical factory, circumstances which make his subsequent scientific achievements and reputation all the more impressive. After a variety of jobs ranging from teaching chemistry, physics and mineralogy in Keilhau to teaching at a boys' school in

16

Epsom, Schoenbein moved to Basel where he was awarded his Doctorate and in 1835 was appointed Professor of Physics and Chemistry at the University of Basel.

Grove conducted a number of experiments between 1839 and 1845, and published a series of papers in the *Philosophical Magazine* and elsewhere recording his progressive discoveries on what he called a 'gas battery' but which is now referred to as the 'fuel cell'.

In his letter to Faraday of 22 October 1842, Grove set out a famous rough sketch of what would later be further developed. Grove went on to present these initial findings more formally in the landmark paper in the *Philosophical Magazine and Journal of Science* for December 1842, *On a Gaseous Voltaic Battery* which also contained a more detailed and well known illustration of the first fuel cells, and described the results of their being combined in a powerful stack of fifty cells. Between then and 1845, Grove published a developing series of papers elaborating upon the ideas and experiments that make up the first fuel cell.

On 11 May 1843 at the Royal Society, Grove read his paper *On the Gas Voltaic Battery – Experiments made with a view of ascertaining the rationale of its action and its application to Eudiometry*, which was also published in the *Philosophical Transactions* for 1843, again, with more detailed illustrations.

By 1845, Grove presented his final, lengthy and detailed paper on the Gas Battery, *On the Gas Voltaic Battery – Voltaic action of Phosphorous, Sulphur and Hydrocarbons*, claiming that …"The results of the above experiments give, I believe, the first instance of the employment of a solid, insoluble non-conductor as the excitant of a continuous voltaic current". By now he was able to give an illustration of a fuel cell with ten cells in two rows, which he speculated could substitute for the water battery, and possibly apply even to the telegraph. The illustrations to this paper had been developed into the beautiful and detailed line drawings that are still used today as the representations of the first working fuel cell.

Bossel makes a powerful case for concluding that Schoenbein made the first discovery of the fuel cell effect in 1838, but that Schoenbein went on to study and interpret the phenomenon; while Grove by 1845 had invented the fuel cell, and was converting scientific knowledge into power generating technology.

Schoenbein and Grove met in England in 1839, when Schoenbein attended the meeting of the British Association for the Advancement of Science in Birmingham as a visiting speaker, and took time to meet Grove and Faraday and others. Schoenbein went to spend the day at Grove's home in London, and apparently the two of them went off by train to visit the skilled instrument maker Francis Watkins where Schoenbein gave orders to build a "Grove cell" to the new design. A few days later Schoenbein, Watkins and Grove watched the formation of gas by electrolysis with the new machine, and the way in which platinum wires melted like wax.

Schoenbein had the "Grove Cell" shipped back to Switzerland, and it was while working on it later in 1839 that he noticed the electrical smell which led him to his discovery of ozone. The final identification of all the characteristics of ozone would take several more years, but this was the route taken by Schoenbein towards its initial discovery.

Also in 1839 Schoenbein and Grove started a correspondence, also published in Bossel's book, that was carried on with greater or lesser regularity, for the rest of their lives. It is a delightful mixture of scientific ideas and observations, growing mutual respect and affection and the occasional career advice. Schoenbein sought (17 April 1840) to dissuade Grove from "…reentering the career of a lawyer. Nature has made you for being a philosopher and you ought to follow her calling." The same letter commented on his discovery of "Ozon".

On 26 October 1841, Grove wrote to Schoenbein about an improved way of processing Daguerrotypes, with a coating of chloride of iodide, also complaining that …"we are in a sad restricted state in England regarding this &other scientific points from the innumerable patents. We scarcely can publish an experiment without risk of a lawsuit." On 20 August 1842, Grove was writing about being the Revising Barrister for a district of Wales, which would occupy him for a month, but …"I have now 3 children & must work for them", a recurring theme in later correspondence.

On 13 March 1846 Grove wrote about Schoenbein's new discovery of gun cotton, and the relative merits of seeking a patent for it or engaging with a manufacturer to help produce it, and Schoenbein's reply the same month gives more details about his remarkable new discovery and its possible applications. Later that year it appears the invention's patent was proceeding, and Schoenbein was writing about its improved capacity over gunpowder to throw 64 pound shells.

By 1 March 1853, Grove was apologising for gaps in his end of the correspondence , but pleading that ..."The fact is that with 6 children a profession some odds & ends of property to attend to & occasionally a few moments devoted to science I am whirled & worried so that my mind is frittered away & I am a nothing doing man because I do so many things." He added that he would rather see Schoenbein's name permanently connected with the element or compound (ozone) than gun cotton, adding "I leave tomorrow for my misery i.e. circuit". In a further letter of 8 October 1857, perhaps after some outbreak of academic bickering, Grove complains that ..."it seems to me the ozone of open rivalry is less noxious than the sulphuretted hydrogen of covered jealousy."

It is a fine correspondence between two distinguished scientists of their day who also come across as very human and appreciative of the other's achievements.

THE DEVELOPMENT OF FUEL CELL POTENTIAL SINCE GROVE

It is 165 years since William Grove sent Faraday his letter about what became known as the fuel cell in October 1842. The potential he unleashed - of highly efficient, clean, quiet energy production on demand - has never seemed more relevant, yet still remains unrealised as a mainstream commercial reality.

The challenges that faced Grove's immediate 19th century successors were in many ways the same challenges facing fuel cell developers today - how to find reliable enough processes, cheap enough components and clean and cheap enough fuels, to compete with cheap, reliable and effective fuels and technologies already in use which have required massive investment in related infrastructure to become established. In Grove's time, the main fuel and technology used were coal and coal-fired centrally generated electricity. 165 years later, coal is still the number one fuel source for power generation, complemented by established and proven nuclear and combined cycle natural gas. For transportation, the incumbent fuel and technology soon after Grove's time became oil, and the internal combustion engine. 165 years later that is still the case. Today there is a rising demand on the power generation and transportation side for alternative energy sources, driven more by concerns about energy security and global warming than by price or performance. However it is not yet clear that the fuel cell industry will be the principal beneficiary of these concerns. Alternative clean technologies such as wind, solar and bio–fuels are competing for larger scale electricity production with less perceived risk that the technology is unproven, while advances in battery technology provide alternatives to fuel cells for portable and consumer electronics applications.

Technical development

The technical development of fuel cells continued at a slow pace in the 19th century. In 1869 Ludwig Mond (1839-1909) and his assistant Carl Langer (d 1935) experimented with a gas battery using coal-derived 'Mond Gas' and a thin perforated platinum electrode. They are generally credited with the first description of their gas battery as a

20

"fuel cell'. Around the same time Charles Alder Wright (1844-1894) and C. Thompson developed a similar fuel cell, but reported problems of gas leakage from one chamber to another. Their conclusion will resonate with many researchers in the field –

> "...our results were sufficiently good to convince us that if the expense of construction were no object, so that large coated plates could be employed, enabling currents of moderate magnitude to be obtained with but small current density, there would be no particular difficulty in constructing [cells] of this kind, competent to yield currents comparable with those derived from ordinary small laboratory batteries; although we concluded that the economical production of powerful currents for commercial purposes by the direct oxidation of combustible gasses did not seem to be a problem likely to be readily solved, chiefly on account of the large appliances that would be requisite."

A French team of Ludwig Paul Cailleteton (1832-1913) and Louis Joseph Colardeau produced an improved version of the Grove fuel cell in 1894, but came to a similar conclusion- that only precious metals would work and therefore that commercial production was uneconomical.

In 1893, Friedrich William Ostwald, one of the founders of the field of physical chemistry, provided much of the theoretical understanding of how fuel cells operate and experimentally determined the interconnected roles of the various components of the fuel cell: electrodes, electrolyte and oxidizing and reducing agents.

In the late 1930s, the Swiss scientist Eric Bauer (1873-1944) and his colleague, H. Preis experimented with solid oxide electrolytes such as yttrium, cerium, lanthanum and tungsten. These electrolytes were not as conductive as they hoped and they experienced unwanted chemical reactions between the electrolytes and various gases, but their research laid the groundwork for the current field of solid oxide fuel cells, and was further advanced in the 1940s by O. K. Davtyan of the Soviet Union.

21

In the late 1930s Francis Thomas Bacon (1904-1992) began researching alkali fuel cells, and in 1939 built a cell using nickel gauze electrodes. He hoped that this might provide a good source of power for Royal Navy submarines. Bacon spent the next 20 years after the war working primarily on alkali fuel cells, resulting in a number of large-scale demonstrations. He also developed a molten carbonate fuel cell. During this period he experimented with various alkali electrolytes, settling on potassium hydroxide. In 1958, he demonstrated an alkali fuel cell using a stack of ten-inch diameter electrodes for Britain's National Research Development Corporation. Bacon's work formed the commercial basis for today's alkali fuel cell development. His patents were also picked up by Pratt & Whitney in the US, who licensed his work for fuel cells supplied to NASA for the Apollo spacecraft program.

The use of fuel cells by NASA in the 1950s and 1960s constituted the first 'commercial' use of fuel cells and was a major factor in focusing attention on their potential. NASA had come to fuel cells by a process of elimination. Batteries were too heavy, solar power (at the time) too expensive, and nuclear power deemed too risky. Fuel cells were also attractive because they produced drinkable water as a by-product. In its initial Gemini space program, NASA backed an early version of the proton exchange membrane fuel cell developed in 1955 by William T. Grubb, a scientist working at GE. Grubb's initial PEM fuel cell was enhanced three years later by another GE chemist, Leonard Niedrach, and the Grubb-Niedrach fuel cell was used by NASA in the Gemini space program. However, NASA was not satisfied with its performance, and, for the Apollo space programme, switched to a Pratt & Whitney-supplied alkali fuel cell that was deemed to be longer lasting. Alkali fuel cells have since been used to power over 100 U.S. space missions (over 80,000 hours) including the space shuttle.

The prominent role of fuel cells in the U.S. space program and the oil embargo in the early 1970s were major factors in driving an acceleration of fuel cell research over the past forty years which has continued despite the collapse of oil prices in the 1980s and 1990s.

This research has evolved into six principal lines based not so much on end use markets as such, but on six different technical types of fuel cell, based on the electrolyte medium. The six principal types of electrolytes are phosphoric acid, alkali, proton exchange measures (PEM), solid oxide, molten carbonate and direct methanol.

The Phosphoric Acid fuel cell (PAFC) was a successor to Grove's sulphuric acid electrolyte, and was developed primarily by G.V. Elmore and H. A. Tanner in the early 1960s. In the mid sixties, the U.S Army tested PAFCs for use with logistics fuel, using an Allis-Chalmers fuel cell. An industry partnership between Pratt & Whitney and the American Gas Association (TARGET) also supported significant research, which led to commercial sales of fuel cells for power plants with capacity up to 5 Megawatts (MW). More recently, Tokyo Electric funded the 11MW "Goi Plant" in Japan using PAFCs. Until 2001, PAFCs had the most significant commercial sales of all fuel cell types, principally for stationary power plants but also for experimental use in transit buses.

Probably the largest amount of research funds have been committed to Proton Exchange Membrane (PEM) fuel cells, largely because they were seen as the most likely type to capture a significant portion of the private car market. PEM Fuel cell technology developed by Grubb and Niedrach at GE powered the Gemini space program in the U.S. GE continued work on PEM Fuel cells and in the mid 1970s developed PEM water electrolysis technology for undersea life support, leading to a U.S. Navy oxygen generation plant. The British Royal Navy adopted this technology in the early 1980s for their submarine fleet. In 1995, Ballard Systems tested PEM Cells in uses in Vancouver and Chicago and in experimental cars made by Daimler Chrysler. Major car makers such as Ford and Volkswagen are testing PEM Vehicles. PEM fuel cells have also been tested in stationary power applications, including Ballard and GPU's 250 KW power plant at the Crane Naval Air Station in Indiana in 1991 and Plug Power's 5KW residential fuel cell demonstration in Albany, NY in 1998.

Solid Oxide Fuel Cells (SOFCs) are receiving significantly increased attention lately, particularly because, at their high operating temperatures, they can use a variety of fuels without poisoning the catalysts and therefore do not depend on pure hydrogen, and on the related challenges and expense of delivering pure hydrogen to the point

23

of use. With their high temperatures and potential high pressures, SOFCs can give the highest fuel efficiency of all fuel cells. In addition to the work of Bauer and Preis in Switzerland and Davyton in the Soviet Union, significant work on solid oxide fuel cells was done at the Central Technical Institute in The Hague, the Consolidation Coal Company in Pennsylvania, and at GE and Westinghouse. SOFCs are currently being tested for large stationary power generation, for residential and commercial combined heat and power (CHP) units and for a variety of niche portable applications, particularly for the military.

Molten Carbonate Fuel Cells are, with SOFCs, one of the highest temperature fuel cells. Their roots, like those of SOFCs, lie in the research of Bauer, Preis and Davtyon into high temperature solid oxide electrolytes. By the late 1950s G.H. J Broers and J.A.A. Ketelaar in the Netherlands and Francis Bacon in Britain had began building on this work and focused on electrolytes of molten carbonate salts as a way around problems of conductivity and unwanted chemical reactions at the time with solid oxides. In the mid 1960s the U.S. Army Mobility Equipment Research and Development Center in Ft. Belvoir tested molten carbonate fuel cells made by Texas Instruments, designed to run on combat gasoline. Molten carbonate fuel cells are currently being developed primarily for large stationary power plants. Ishikawajima Heavy Industries in Japan successfully operated a 1,000 KW molten carbonate fuel cell power generator in the early 1990s and at least 10 Japanese companies are currently working on MCFCs. In 1996, Fuel Cell Energy (then the Energy Research Corp) demonstrated a 2 MW MCFC plant in Santa Clara, California, and now has over 50 MCFC plants operating. Fuel Cell Energy has also developed small scale power plants which use a hybrid MCFC fuel cell and gas turbine.

The newest type of fuel cell is the Direct Methanol Fuel Cell (DMFC). This is similar to a PEM fuel cell, except that a catalyst on the DMFC cathode draws hydrogen from liquid methanol, eliminating the need for a fuel cell reformer and allowing pure methanol to be used as a fuel. This has opened the potential for direct methanol fuel cells with small methanol cartridges, to be used as substitutes for batteries in consumer electronics, including laptops, cell phones and electronic personal organisers.

This flurry of fuel cell development activity, particular over the past twenty years, suggests that governments, academic organizations and above all private sector companies continue to believe strongly in the long term potential of fuel cells despite their slow commercial adoption cycle to date. There are five principal reasons for their optimism about the commercial prospects for fuel cells.

World oil prices

World oil prices have risen sharply over the past decade from their lows in the late eighties and nineties. Oil prices are notoriously hard to forecast accurately, as shown by the long standing debate on whether or not oil production has peaked. Much of the current world price reflects uncertainties on the reliability of supply, rather than excess demand, but these supply uncertainties show no sign of abating, while demand is growing strongly, driven particularly by the rapid industrialization of the developing world. Even at today's oil price, fuel cells, despite their superior fuel efficiency, are not price competitive with oil or coal on any unsubsidized application, but improvements in materials design and large-scale manufacturing are expected to bring fuel cell prices down sufficiently to be competitive without subsidies within five to ten years.

Energy security

Beyond the price of oil, there is rapidly increasing political concern in most of the developed world for energy security, particularly given rising instability in the Middle East, increasing use of energy as a political weapon by Russia, Venezuela and a number of other oil producing countries, and rapidly increasing competition from China and India for access to long term energy supplies. Fuel cells address the issue of energy security in two ways. First and foremost by relying primarily on domestic supplies of hydrogen; secondly by achieving fuel cell efficiency that is substantially greater than that of internal combustion engines (40-50% for most fuel cell types and up to 85% for high temperature fuel cells including the heating function).

Climate change

Fuel cells directly address the challenge of global warming and urban pollution. When hydrogen is the fuel, the emissions of carbon dioxide, nitrogen oxide, sulphur oxides and particulate matter associated with fossil fuel combustion, are nil. When fossil fuels are reformed into hydrogen in fuel cells, these emissions are a fraction of that produced by fossil fuel combustion.

The increased focus on energy security and climate change is prompting increasing political action to support alternative 'clean technologies' in general and fuel cells in particular. These include heavy subsidies for clean electricity, particularly in Germany, the rest of Europe and Japan, an increase in national legal provisions requiring that a percentage of 'grid' power be derived from such clean technologies, 'low emissions' passenger car requirements, ever increasing air quality standards and direct fuel cell development subsidies (in the United States, Europe and Japan).

Distributed Generation

There is a worldwide trend towards distributed generation of electricity (electricity production at the point of use, rather than depending upon large power stations), and this is driven by deregulation and direct commercial purchasing in the United States and Europe, and by compelling economics in the developing world. There are some similarities with the phenomenon of cell phones bypassing landline telephone development. Fuel cell industries are once again not the only beneficiary of this trend, and must compete, for instance, with micro turbines, but the trend plays to the strength of fuel cells, particularly as a natural source of combined heat and power (CHP) for higher temperature fuel cells.

Mobile consumer electronics

The huge surge in worldwide demand for mobile consumer electronics devices (cellphones, personal organizers, laptop computers and so on), coupled with the advent of mobile broadband, is leading to demand for exponential increases in battery life. Direct Methanol fuel cells could be a major beneficiary of this trend.

This combination of trends suggests that the long term potential for fuel cells is substantial. The largest long term market potential continues to be in distributed generation (including CHP), and in primary power for cars, trucks and buses, but there also appear to be substantial higher priced and potentially nearer term specialist markets, particularly in various forms of auxiliary or back up power, including for military uses.

The challenge for fuel cells developers is to overcome the obstacles of cost and reliability that have so far inhibited the development of any meaningful commercial markets for 165 years. One of the biggest challenges remains the question of who is to pay for the hydrogen distribution infrastructure required for those fuel cells that use pure hydrogen. Estimates of this infrastructure cost for passenger cars in the US alone are in the region of $12-20 billion. Another significant cost hurdle is the use of highly expensive material in the construction of many types of fuel cells, particularly the platinum used in PEM fuel cells. The frustration of the capital markets with fuel cells can be seen in the fact that nearly all of the huge volume of "clean technology" financing in the past five years (approaching $6 billion per year in the US alone), is going into investments in wind power, solar energy and bio-fuels, which, as established and proven technologies are seen as having much less 'technology' risk than fuel cells. Private and public fuel cell funding has been affected both by the perception that the technology is unproven and therefore more risky and also by the after-effect of the substantial losses incurred on fuel cell funding at the height of the technology boom in 1999 and 2000, when funding was based on wildly optimistic assumptions on the timing of commercialization. Despite these setbacks, funding for fuel cell development continues to be available, albeit at a fraction of the investment in other "alternative energy technologies". It is coming from a combination of public sector and academic sources, continued spending on research and development by large corporations, particularly by users such as power companies, car companies, and appliance manufacturers, and to some extent from venture capital and investors in clean technology.

How then to assess Grove's legacy in the later development of his fuel cell invention? It is surely a 'tale of two cities'. On the one hand, there has been over-promotion, continued failure to live up to the promises of timing for commercialization, and no material commercial markets have developed in 165 years. On the other hand, economic and political conditions have never been so favourable in the whole of that 165 year period, there is every likelihood that these conditions will only become more favourable in the next few decades, and a highly active worldwide development effort has accelerated rapidly in the past 20 years, and has made substantial technological progress. These factors make it possible, but not certain, that fuel cells will, at last, become a major factor in worldwide energy and transportation markets, instead of just a curiosity.

THE CORRELATION OF PHYSICAL FORCES

Grove is known today almost entirely for his scientific work as the 'father of the fuel cell'. A late photograph of a bewhiskered Victorian gentleman, or perhaps an engraving of the first Grove fuel cell or Grove battery, give those attending a fuel cell conference a fleeting glimpse of the work of a lifetime. But in his own lifetime, Grove's reputation was based in large part upon his lectures at the London Institution, especially those given in 1842, which he went on to publish in 1843 in the Literary Gazette as *The Correlation of Physical Forces*.

This work went to many separate editions, and despite some detractors, attracted widespread admiration from Grove's contemporaries in the scientific and non-scientific fields alike, so any account of Grove's professional achievements is incomplete without some account of his major book. However, this is a sample, rather than a scientific review, and scientists may prefer to consult the source.

In *The Correlation of Physical Forces*, Grove set out to explore the relationship which he believed existed between the different aspects of 'forces', which he described as 'Light, Heat, Electricity, Magnetism, Motion and Chemical Affinity'. In the original lectures, and progressively through the new editions of the work, he drew on not only his own experiments, but also referred to the work of many leading authorities in their own fields. The work of Joule, Montgolfier, Faraday, Davy, Bunsen, Volta, Seguin, Carnot, Herschel, Franklin, Becquerel, Newton, Schoenbein and many others are freely referred to where their work helped to establish a point or sharpen an argument.

Grove himself had his own view as to the originality of the work. In the preface to the 1867 fifth edition he said that –

> "...I have been regarded by many rather as the historian of the progress made in this branch of thought than as one who has had anything to do with its initiation. Everyone is but a poor judge where he is himself interested, and I therefore write with diffidence, but it would be affecting an indifference which I do not feel if I did not state that I believe myself to have been the first who introduced this subject as a generalised system of

philosophy, and continued to enforce it in my lectures and writings for many years, during which it met with the opposition usual and proper to novel ideas."

Grove argued that light, heat, electricity, magnetism, motion and chemical-affinity were all convertible "material affections", and that "assuming either as the cause, one of the others will be the effect: thus heat may be said to produce electricity, electricity to produce heat; magnetism to produce electricity..." and so on. He argued that these "affections of matter which constitute the main objects of experimental physics" were all correlative, or have a reciprocal dependence. Neither, taken abstractedly, could be said to be the independent cause of the others, but either may produce or be convertible into any of the others; and further that ..."the same must hold good of other forces, it being an irresistible inference from observed phenomena that a force cannot originate otherwise than by devolution from some pre-existing force or forces."

He was propounding this theory at a time when he was obliged to admit that ..."we are totally unacquainted with the ultimate generating power of each of them, and probably shall ever remain so..." so "we must humbly refer their causation to one omnipresent influence, and content ourselves with studying their effects and developing by experiment their mutual relations." At several points in *The Correlation of Physical Forces* Grove makes similar remarks about the unlikelihood of ever knowing the answers to some difficult scientific conundrum, which might begin to suggest that his own contribution was more in the nature of careful step by step experimentation and observation than cantering ahead with free-ranging speculation and theorising.

In the Preface, Grove refers to the way in which his legal career came to displace his short burst of scientific originality –

> ..."The short and irregular intervals which my profession permits me to devote to science so prevent the continuity of attention necessary for the proper evolution of a train of thought..."

But he also referred to the encouragement that he had received from those whose opinion he valued in publishing the lectures as an Essay …"and the, I trust pardonable, wish not to let some favourite thoughts of my use lose all connection with my name…"

Motion

In considering motion in the first part of the Essay, Grove asked …"what becomes of force when motion is arrested or impeded by the counter-motion of another body?" and he suggested that rather than the motion being lost or destroyed, the heat which resulted from friction or percussion was a continuation of the force which was previously associated with the moving body.

As with the other forces, Grove related his own answers to questions by reference to experiment. He noted that if a body moved in fluid, although some heat was generated, it was trifling, because the particles of the fluid themselves moved, and thereby continued the motion communicated to them –

> "As the converse of this proposition, it should follow that the more rigid the bodies impinging on each other the greater should be the amount of heat developed by friction, and so we find it. Flint, steel, hard stones, glass, and metals are those bodies which give the greatest amount of heat from friction or percussion; while water, oil &c., give little or no heat, and from the ready mobility of their particles lessen its development when interposed between rigid moving bodies. Thus, if we oil the axles of wheels, we have more rapid motion of the bodies themselves, but less heat…"

Friction, according to this view was "simply impeded motion". And after a lecture or chapter considering different experimental approaches of motion and its effects, Grove summarises the ways in which motion can directly produce heat and electricity, which can then produce magnetism. Motion can produce light, either through friction or electricity –

31

"In the decompositions or compositions which the terminal points proceeding from the conductors of an electrical machine develop when immersed in different chemical media, we get the production of *chemical affinity* by electricity, of which motion is the initial source."

Finally, Grove argued, motion could be reproduced by the forces which emanated from it –

"…thus, the divergence of the electrometer, the revolution of the electric wheel, the deflection of the magnetic needle, are, when resulting from frictional electricity, palpable movements reproduced by the intermediate modes of force, which have themselves been originated by motion."

Heat

Grove's lectures on heat went on to explore and describe a variety of experiments on solids, liquids, gases and relative temperatures –

"Now place the thermometer at 100^0, successively on one oz. of water at 32^0, and in one of ice at 32^0; we shall find in the former case it will be lowered only to 54^0, and in the latter to 32^0; apply this to the doctrine of repulsive force, and we get a satisfactory explanation…"

If the thermometer had been placed in an unlimited quantity of water, the mercury would have fallen to the temperature of the surrounding water at 32^0; but with the quantity of water limited, the mercury would lose more repulsive power by the ice than the water.

Grove went on to describe heat as …"simply a communicable molecular repulsive force…", a view which he maintained was supported by many of the phenomena to which the term specific or relative heat is applied. He went on to consider the different ways in which metals and other substances expanded when heated or contracted when cooled. He later argued that –

"Though I am obliged, in order to be intelligible, to talk of heat as an entity, and of its conduction, radiation &c., yet these expressions are, in fact, inconsistent with the dynamic theory which regards heat as motion and nothing else; thus conduction would simply be a progressive dilation or motion of the particles of the conducting substance, radiation an undulation or motion of the particles through which the heat is said to be transmitted, &c.; and it is a strong argument in favour of this theory, that for every diversity in the physical character of bodies, and for every change in the structure and arrangement of particles in the same body, a change is apparent in the thermal effects. Thus gold conducts heat, or transmits the motion called heat, more readily than copper, copper than iron, iron than lead, and lead than porcelain, &c."

Grove described a variety of ways in which heat produces both electricity, and light, and considered the relation of radiation to absorption, and absorptive and reflective powers. He described an experiment of showing how more intense heat produced light by bringing a platinum wire to the point of visible ignition by heating it with a voltaic battery in a dark room.

For 'chemical-affinity' Grove noted that if a substance capable of supporting intense heat but incapable of being acted upon by water or either of its elements, such as platinum or iridium, was raised to an intense heat and then immersed in water, bubbles of permanent gas were produced, which proved to be a mixture of both oxygen and hydrogen. He noted that oxygen and hydrogen combined to form water at a temperature of about 800^0, but that they appeared to separate into the two gases at about 2386^0.

The importance of Grove's experiments and conclusions in this area is underlined by the reflection that so much of it was directly applicable to his work on batteries, and also to his work on fuel cells. His years in the laboratory and in preparation for the lecture hall were part of the jigsaw that made the foundation for the work that was remembered.

Grove considered Carnot's essay of 1824, which regarded the mechanical power produced by heat as resulting from a transfer of heat from one point to another, without any ultimate loss of heat. He applied this to the working of a steam engine, with the heat from the furnace expanding the water in a boiler, raising the piston, and then being cooled and contracted by the working of the condenser. He compared the work done by Watt, and Desormes, on the heat in a steam engine and the heat required to maintain a vapour in the piston.

Grove's studies and readings on heat, and his view of it as a continuation of motion, are a central part of his overall work on physics. Like the other 'forces', Grove was constitutionally disinclined to see heat as a force on its own. He saw it instead as a reflection or cause of other forces –

> "As neither from observation, nor from deduction, can we fix or conjecture any boundary to the universe of stellar orbs, as each advance in telescopic power gives us a new shell, so to speak, or stars, we may regard our globe, in the limit, as surrounded by a sphere of matter radiating heat, light, and possibly other forces."

Electricity

It is some measure of Grove's reputation in this field that he was introduced as a lecturer at the London Institution by Faraday himself, and it must be wondered why Faraday would have done that had he not respected Grove's own contribution and experimental experience in the fields of electricity and other aspects of physics.

In his lecture or chapter on electricity, Grove considered the phenomenon of induction, and Faraday's own work in the area –

> "When an electrified conductor is brought near another which is not electrified, the latter becomes electrified by influence or induction, as it is termed, the nearest parts of each of these two bodies exhibiting states of electricity of the contrary denominations. Until this subject was investigated by Faraday, the intervening non-conducting body or dielectric was supposed to be purely negative, and the effect was attributed to the repulsion at a distance of the electrical fluid. Faraday showed

that these effects differed greatly according to the dielectric that was interposed. Thus they were more exalted with sulphur than with shellac; more with shellac than with glass, &c."

Grove's own experiments also dealt with electrolysis, and it is hard to go back and put yourself in the position of these pioneers, who had to work out each aspect from first principles, and to realise how much of their work is really the basis for modern electronics, lighting, computing, fuel cell production and so much else -

"...chemical action or electrolysis may, as I have shown, be transmitted by induction across a dielectric substance, such as glass, but apparently only while the glass is being charged with electricity. A wire passing through and hermetically sealed into a glass tube, a short portion only projecting, is made to dip into water to an equal depth with that within it; the wire and another similar wire dipping into the outer water are made to communicate metallically with the powerful electrical machine known as Rhumkorf's coil; bubbles of gas instantly ascend from the exposed portions of the wires, but cease after a certain time, and are renewed when, after an interval of separation, the coil is again connected with the wires."

Grove's interest in the principles of photography, and its scientific basis rather than its aesthetic potential, is underlined by his description of experiments in which he electrified a glass plate and then 'etched' an impression of a coin placed upon it into the underlying glass. This led him on to described his own experiments with photographic techniques, coating the glass with a film of iodised collodion "in the manner usually adopted for photographic purposes", then in a dark room immersing in a solution of nitrate of silver, exposing to the light for a few seconds, and washing with pyrogallic acid and fixing with hyposulphite of sulphur.

But while the earliest photographers might have been principally concerned with the nature of the image that they had obtained by these techniques, Grove was more concerned with the molecular changes in the materials affected by this combination of electricity, chemicals and light. From these experiments he came to regard electricity not, as many of his contemporaries did, as some sort of fluid, but ..."produced by an emission of the material itself from whence they issue, and a molecular action of the gas, or intermedium, through or across which they are transmitted." This observation, while not a theory in itself, was surely very significant as a 'way of thinking' which must have helped condition the work undertaken by many others in the field. Grove underlined the point by reference to the colours of electric sparks –

> "The colour of the electric spark, or of the whole voltaic arc (i.e. the flame which plays between the terminal points of a powerful voltaic battery), is dependent upon the substance of the metal, subject to certain modifications of the intermedium: thus, the electric spark or arc from zinc is blue; from silver, green; from iron red and scintillating; precisely the colours afforded by these metals in their ordinary combustion. A portion of the metal is also found to be actually transmitted with every electric or voltaic discharge...the metallic particles emitted by the electrodes or terminals can be readily collected, tested or even weighed."

And from this he drew the highly important conclusion –

> "It would thus appear that the electrical discharge arises, at least in part, from an actual repulsion and severance of the electrified matter itself, which flies off at the points of least resistance."

He described the voltaic arc itself as properly neither ignition nor combustion. It was not ignition because the matter of the terminals did not become properly incandescent, but he noted a physical separation and partial transfer from one electrode to another, partly through a vaporous state. And it was not combustion, because the 'phenomena' would take place independently of atmospheric air, oxygen or gas of the kinds usually required to support combustion. What then actually occurred, for example when fine black zinc powder was deposited on the sides of the receiver after a voltaic discharge between two zinc terminals?

Grove concluded that the voltaic discharge consists of the material itself of which the terminals are composed, and noted that a peculiar effect of rotation of light occurred when iron was used as electric terminals, with the magnetic character of the metal causing the molecules to rotate under the influence of the voltaic current. He applied these principles to batteries –

> "If we increase the number of reduplications in a voltaic series, we increase the length of the arc, and also increase its intensity or power of overcoming resistance. With a battery consisting of a limited number, say 100 reduplications, the discharge will not pass from one terminal to the other without first bringing them into contact, but if we increase the number of cells to 400 or 500, the discharge will pass from one terminal to the other before they are brought into contact."

To achieve the most powerful batteries, therefore, Grove reduced the size of the plates of the battery, but increased the number of reduplications, a pattern which can be seen to some extent reflected in the early illustrations of Grove's nitric acid battery and the earliest representations of his fuel cell. Grove had experimented with all sorts and sizes of batteries and electrical apparatus, and had closely observed their effects. He noted that, for example, when a fine platinum wire was hermetically sealed in a glass tube, and the end of the tube and wire ground to a flat surface so as to expose only a section of the wire, after an electrical discharge was made through the wire for some time, the end of the wire itself wore away, and ended before the end of the glass, while platinum was observed as discharged around the point of the electrode. This kind of observation helped Grove to conclude that electricity was not a 'fluid' but a form of excitation of the molecules of the matter of the electrodes and the matter through which it passed. He noted other phenomena in further experiments with electricity –

> "Let discharges from a Leyden jar or battery be passed through a platinum wire, too thick to be fused by the discharges, and free from constraint, it will be found that the wire is shortened; it has undergone a molecular change, and apparently been acted on by a force transverse to its length. If the discharges be continued, it gradually gathers up in small irregular bends or convolutions. So with voltaic electricity: place a platinum wire in a trough of porcelain, so that when fused it shall retain its

position as a wire, and then ignite it by a voltaic battery. As it reaches the point of fusion it will snap asunder, showing a contraction in length, and consequently a distension or increase in its transverse dimensions. Perform the same experiment with a lead wire, which can be more readily kept in a state of fusion, and follow it, as it contracts, by the terminal wires of the battery; it will be seen to gather up in nodules, which press on each other like a string of beads of a soft material which have been longitudinally compressed."

The characteristic effects of electricity upon wires can be seen today in the wearing of filaments in electric light bulbs, which is still the main determinant of their length of use. Grove noted the different conductivity for electricity of different substances, and if different forms of the same substance –

"Carbon, in a transparent crystalline state, as diamond, is as perfect a non-conductor as we know; while in an opaque amorphous state, as graphite or charcoal, it is one of the best conductors: thus in one state it transmits light and stops electricity, in the other it transmits electricity and stops light."

He described experiments which he had designed himself to establish and try to measure the loss of electricity, or its conversion into mechanical power. In describing electrical ignition, Grove returned to the experimental home ground of batteries on which so much of his future fame was to be based –

"In the phenomenon of electrical ignition, as shown by a heated conjunctive wire, the relation of force and resistance, and the correlative character of the two forces, electricity and heat, are strikingly demonstrated. Let a thin wire of platinum join the terminals of a voltaic battery of suitable power, the wire will be ignited, and a certain amount of chemical action will take place in the cells of the battery – a definite quantity of zinc being dissolved and of hydrogen eliminated in a given time. If now the platinum wire be immersed in water, the heat will, from the circulating currents of the liquid, be more rapidly dissipated, and we shall instantly find that the chemical action in the battery will be increased, more zinc will be dissolved, and more hydrogen eliminated at the same time; the heat being conveyed away by the water; more chemical action is required to generate it, just as more fuel is required in proportion as evaporation is more rapid."

Grove's treatment of electricity in this lecture or chapter is characterised by quiet authority, long experience, personal experimentation and considerable originality. He must have played a significant part in correcting the view then current of electricity as a fluid, and its identification as a force affecting the molecular matter of electrical terminals and the matter through which electricity is passed. This, and his ground-breaking work on batteries, formed a significant part of his overall contribution to the science of physics.

Light

In his treatment of light and refraction, Grove demonstrated how for him the real interest in photography was first and foremost scientific rather than artistic. His lecture or chapter has almost ten pages comparing the relative scientific techniques used by Fox Talbot and Daguerre.

These processes, Grove said, were "new and surprising at the period when these Lectures were delivered" [1842-1843] but "photographic processes have now become familiar, not only to the cultivator of science, but to the artist and amateur." He reasserted his scientific interest in the subject by declaring that …"the important point for consideration here is that light will chemically or molecularly affect matter." As he said –

> "At my Lectures in 1843, I showed an experiment by which the production of all the other models of force by light is exhibited: I may here shortly describe it. A prepared daguerreotype plate is enclosed in a box filled with water, having a glass front with a shutter over it. Between this glass and the plate is a gridiron of silver wire; the plate is connected with one extremity of a Breguet's helix – an elegant instrument, formed by a coil of two metals, the unequal expansion of which indicates slight changes

39

in temperature – the other extremities of the galvanometer and helix are connected by a wire, and the needles brought to zero. As soon as a beam of either daylight or oxyhydrogen light is, by raising the shutter, permitted to impinge upon the plate, the needles are deflected. Thus light being the initiating force, we get *chemical action* on the plate, *electricity* circulating through the wires, *magnetism* in the coil, *heat* in the helix and *motion* in the needles."

Grove considered the relationship between light and heat in a variety of simple experiments –

"Let two vessels of water, the content of the one clear and transparent, of the other tinged by some colouring matter, be suspended in a summer's sun; in a very short time a notable difference of temperature will be observed, the coloured having become much hotter than the clear liquid....So, with regard to the medium transmitting the influence: a greenhouse may have its temperature considerably varied by changing the glass of which its roof is made."

Grove stated that in his Lectures of 1842 his view had been that the nature of light was consistent with its "resulting from a vibration or motion of the molecules of matter itself, rather than the specific ether pervading it." In later editions of the work, he took account of the similar work by the celebrated mathematician Leonard Euler. Despite opposition to these ideas, Grove came back to his view that the actions of light were an instance of "ordinary matter acting from particle to particle", and he cited in support the similarities of results in Faraday's experiments on electrical induction and his own on the voltaic arc. He also cited the work of Becquerel, who went on to pioneer some aspects of the science of radiation. As with electricity, he was arguing against a body of scientific opinion which held light to be some sort of matter or fluid in itself, and in favour of the view that it represented some effect of motion or force on molecular particles of the matter through which it travelled.

After touching on the experimental work of Pasteur on crystallised salts of paratartaric acid, Grove returned to photography, as evidencing the ways in which "light alters the structure of matter submitted to it," and thence to speculations on the relationship of light to motion.

Grove then dealt with the counter argument that –

>...—"if light, heat, electricity &c., be affections of ordinary matter, then matter must be supposed to be everywhere where these phenomena are apparent, and consequently there can be no vacuum.
>
> These forces are transmitted through what are called vacua, or through interplanetary spaces, where matter, if it exist, must be in a highly attenuated state."

This led him to consider the contemporary difficulties in achieving a perfect vacuum, and that led him on to speculations about the nature of "outer space", suggesting (by reference to Sir W. Herschel, Newton and others) that –

> "Ether, or the highly-attentuated matter existing in the interplanetary spaces, being an expansion of some or all of these atmospheres, or of the most volatile portions of them, would thus furnish matter for the transmissions of the modes of motion which we call light, heat &c.; and possibly minute portions of these atmospheres may, by gradual changes, pass from planet to planet, forming a link of material communication between the distant monads of the universe."

It was to take Einstein to be able to explain the electro magnetic characteristics of light. Grove was correct in instinctively resisting the notion of electricity and light as some form of fluid, but he was unable to provide full explanations for something that as yet lacked Einstein's theoretical basis.

Magnetism

Grove began his lecture or essay on magnetism by reference to Faraday's important discovery that magnetism would produce electricity, but he said that magnetism was directive but not of itself motive. It changed the direction of molecules in soft iron like the wind on a weather-vane. With hard iron or steel, as with a stiff weather-vane, it took more magnetic force to change the molecules' direction (as if requiring a stronger wind to turn the weather-vane), but when so polarised, these substances could not be affected by a feeble current of electricity. They themselves originate an electric current.

Grove noted that –

> "Since these lectures were delivered, Faraday has discovered a remarkable effect of magnetic force in occasioning the deflection of a ray of polarised light."

He went on to describe how –

> "I have, since the first edition of this Essay was published, communicated to the Royal Society a paper by which I think I have satisfactorily proved, that whenever any metal susceptible to magnetism is magnetised or demagnetised, its temperature is raised. This was shown, first, by subjecting a bar of iron, nickel or cobalt to the influence of a powerful electro-magnet, which was rapidly magnetised and de-magnetised in reverse directions, the electro-magnet itself being kept cool by cisterns of water, so that the magnetic metal subjected to the influence of magnetism was raised to a higher temperature than the electro-magnet itself, and could not, therefore, have acquired its increased temperature by conduction or radiation of heat from the electro-magnet; and secondly by rotating a permanent steel magnet with its poles opposite to a bar of iron, and thermo-electric pile being placed opposite the latter."

Overall, however, Grove has less to say about detailed experiments about magnetism than on electricity, and he appears to have seen it more as a form of 'force' which he was obliged to address in view of his perceived relation of different forces to each other.

Chemical Affinity

By chemical affinity, Grove meant the 'force' by which dissimilar 'bodies' tend to unite and form compounds generally differing in character from their constituents, and he admitted that this was the force of which least was known at that time.

The way in which Grove observed chemical reactions therefore tended to be experimental and sometimes tentative, and yet the results of his curiosity gave us the fuel cell –

> "If gold be immersed in hydrochloric acid, no chemical action takes place. If gold be immersed in nitric acid, no chemical action takes place; but mix the two acids, and the immersed gold is chemically attacked and dissolved: this is an ordinary chemical action, the result of a double chemical affinity. In hydrochloric acid, which is composed of chlorine and hydrogen, the affinity of chlorine for gold being less than its affinity for hydrogen, no change takes place; but when the nitric acid is added, this latter containing a great quantity of oxygen in a state of feeble combination, the affinity of oxygen for hydrogen opposes that of hydrogen for chlorine, and then the affinity of the latter for gold is enabled to act, the gold combines with the chlorine and chloride of gold remains in solution in the liquid."

Grove demonstrated the practical applications of his experiments in chemical affinity by reference to the batteries which he had himself invented –

> "There are few, if any, chemical actions which cannot be experimentally made to produce electricity: the oxidation of metals, the burning of combustibles, the combination of oxygen and hydrogen &c., may all be made sources of electricity. The common mode in which the electricity of the voltaic battery is generated is by the chemical action of water upon zinc: this action is increased by adding certain acids to the water, which enable it to act more powerfully upon the zinc, or in some cases act themselves upon it; and one of the most powerful chemical actions known – that of nitric acid upon oxidable metals – is

that which produces the most powerful voltaic battery, a combination which I made known in the year 1839…"

This was Grove's nitric acid battery, whose powerful chemical actions and nitric acid fumes made operators of telegraphs ill. Later in the same chapter, Grove described the chemical changes in a voltaic battery and the production of oxygen and hydrogen produced, in the proportion in which they form water, when the two platinum terminals of the voltaic battery were immersed in water. He went on to consider how heat, light, magnetism and motion, as other 'forces' could be produced by chemical affinity. In discussing chemical combinations, he referred in passing to the discovery by his friend and correspondent Dr Schoenbein of gun cotton.

Grove showed himself as finding a way towards wider conclusions about his work on chemical affinity –

> "The doctrine of definite combining proportions, which so beautifully serves to relate chemistry to voltaic electricity, led to the atomic theory, which, though adopted in its universality by a large majority pf chemists, presents great difficulties when extended to all chemical combinations."

A later chapter dealt briefly with 'Other Modes of Force', including catalysis, or chemical reactions induced by the presence of a foreign body, and the application of his theories, and the experiments of others, in diverse fields such as Professor Mateucci's work on electrical stimuli and nerves (presented to the Royal Society in 1850).

Concluding Remarks

Grove tried to draw together his thoughts on these topics in his last chapter –

> "The term Correlation, which I selected as the title of my Lectures in 1843, strictly interpreted, means a necessary mutual or reciprocal dependence of two ideas, inseparable even in mental conception: thus the idea of height cannot exist without

44

involving the idea of its correlate, depth; the idea of parent
cannot exist without involving the idea of offspring."

He explained and commended the unusual use of the term in its
application to physics. Again, his work reflected considerable
limitations to contemporary knowledge –

"Probably man will never know the ultimate structure of matter
or the minutiae of molecular actions…"

In the expression of these limitations, it becomes necessary to see *The
Correlation of Physical Forces* not so much as a complete theory as an
expression of detailed contemporary knowledge, and a way of helping
his contemporaries to categorise, think about and explain the
phenomena that they were themselves learning about at an ever
increasing rate. The book and its author need to be seen in the context
of their times, and the quite extraordinary explosion of scientific
knowledge represented by the 19th century. At the beginning of that
century, the height of medical skill was amputation without anaesthetic;
by its close there had been huge strides in vaccination, anaesthetics and
all manner of other medical advances. So with physics and chemistry,
engineering, mechanics, biology and so many other fields. Britain was
moving from a settled agrarian economy to the centre of the industrial
revolution. Scientists were turning from the gentlemen amateurs or
'natural philosophers' of the 18th century into the serious minded
explorers like Faraday with whom Grove worked so closely. Inventors
like Daguerre and Fox Talbot were claiming whole new sciences and
industries from their pioneering work.

In the midst of this scientific ferment, Grove was struggling for some
kind of order in scientific thought –

"In investigating the relation of the different forces, I have in
turn taken each one as the initial force or starting-point, and
endeavoured to show how the force thus arbitrarily selected
could mediately or immediately produce and be merged into the
others: but it will be obvious to those who have attentively
considered the subject, and brought their minds into a general
accordance with the views I have submitted to them, that no

45

force can, strictly speaking, be initial, as there must be some anterior force which produced it: we cannot create force or motion any more than we can create matter."

He did not exaggerate the importance of his writings –

"That the theoretical portions of this essay are open to objection I am fully conscious. I cannot, however, but think that the fair way to test a theory is to compare it with other theories, and to see whether upon the whole the balance of probability is in its favour. Were a theory open to no objection it would cease to be a theory, and would become a law; and were we not to theorise, or to take generalised views of natural phenomena until those generalisations were sure and unobjectionable – in other words, were laws – science would be lost in a complex mass of unconnected observations, which would probably never disentangle themselves."

He tried to avoid hasty generalisation, but was equally determined to try to avoid wasting time by simply collecting elaborate observations and "leaving the subject to which they refer in greater obscurity than that in which it was involved at their commencement." As he put it –

"As the knowledge of any particular science develops itself, our views of it become more simple; hypotheses, or the introduction of supposititious views, are more and more dispensed with; words become applicable more directly to the phenomena, and, losing the hypothetic meaning which they necessarily possessed at their reception, acquire a secondary sense, which brings more immediately to our minds the facts of which they are indices. The scaffolding has served its purpose. The hypothesis fades away, and a theory, or generalised view of phenomena, more independent of supposition, but still full of gaps and difficulties, takes its place. This in turn, should the science continue to progress, either gives place to a more simple and wider generalisation, or becomes, by the removal of objections, established as a law."

..."Where to draw the line – where to say thus far may we go, and no farther, in any particular class of analogies or relations which Nature presents to us...I have throughout endeavoured to discard the hypotheses of subtle or occult entities; if in this endeavour some of my views have been adopted upon insufficient data, I still hope that this essay will not prove valueless."

This was a scientist and a writer who would conclude that "Causation is the will, Creation the act, of God". He knew his limits, and the limits of contemporary knowledge, for which in many areas he did not expect or foresee the discovery of scientific answers. He knew better than to claim an authority for his mixture of hypothesis and theory that it could not carry. But he sensed the value at a time of scientific ferment of having a better organised way of thinking rather than a collection of minutely observed 'islands' of scientific experimental reporting. It is not surprising that the reaction of his contemporaries was mixed, with a few finding *The Correlation of Physical Forces* unpersuasive, while many others found it to be remarkable and authoritative. The fact that at the time of his death it was still the basis for much of Grove's fame and renown as a scientist suggests that those who approved and found it to be of benefit were in a large majority.

Even those who derived little benefit or understanding from the detailed exposition of the "theory" of Correlation must have found much unarguable, careful work describing with Grove's quiet authority the experimental work he had undertaken. The authority which enabled him to dissent from the view of electricity as a 'fluid', to describe the scientific basis of the earliest photography, to describe the electrical and chemical processes at work in the batteries that bore his name. There are many expressions in this work of the scientific originality of the inventor of the fuel cell, and those with an interest in the history of science would be well advised to read *The Correlation of Physical Forces* for themselves.

Grove was keenly interested in all aspects of scientific activity, and by chance the years he spent as a young man carrying out original research and spreading the word on scientific matters by lectures and articles happened to coincide with the pioneering work on developing photography which was taking place in France and in England in the 1830's and 1840's.

In France the most notable figure was Louis Daguerre who, in partnership with Joseph Nicéphone Niépce, invented the Daguerreotype, a positive photograph using an amalgam image on polished silver which was mainly used to produce small portraits in padded cases. Daguerre's process was announced to the Académie des Sciences in Paris in January 1839. His portraits were popular for some 10 years but the process was difficult to carry out, while for a time the long exposures needed limited them to static subjects. The intrepid travellers who wished to take Daguerreotypes of scenes in remote countries also had problems taking with them very bulky and heavy equipment. But initially Daguerre's invention was very successful and in the hands of experts produced very elegant results. In March 1841 Richard Beard opened the first Daguerreoptype portrait studio in Regent Street.

One of the well known Daguerrotypists for whom Grove sat as a subject was John Jabez Edwin Mayall, originally known as Jabez Meal. Mayall was a British Daguerrotypist who started work in America, and later returned to London to open 'The American Daguerrotype Institution', bcoming a photographer to Queen Victoria and other well known figures, opening studios in London and Brighton.

Grove was keenly interested in Daguerre's work and found a way to etch the plates so that prints of them could be made. What he described as the secret of this process was "to make the Daguerreotype the anode of a Voltaic combination, in a solution which will not of itself attack either silver or mercury, but of which, when electrolysed, the anion will attack thee metals unequally." " This idea" he wrote, " occurred to me soon after the publication of Daguerre's process; but then being in the country and unable to procure any plates, I allowed the matter to sleep; and other occupations prevented for some time any recurrence to it." In due course, however, he decided to experiment on the lines of his original notion, and his friend Mr. Gassiot obtained for him a supply of the plates. This led to a paper by Grove read to the London Electrical Society on 17August 1841 entitled "On a Voltaic Process for Etching Daguerreotypes Plates."

Meanwhile in England photographic research was being undertaken by William Henry Fox Talbot, described by the National Trust as " a gentleman scholar of considerable means and social standing" living at Lacock Abbey in Wiltshire. He was a remarkable polymath who was for a time an MP and studied all manner of things – mathematics, chemistry, classics, philosophy, botany, Assyriology, and archaeology - but is best known as the principal inventor of photography. Talbot experimented with what he called "photogenic drawing" and in 1835 produced the earliest known photographic negative on paper. This was a photogenic drawing of an oriel window at Lacock Abbey. The idea of photography had come to him when he was on holiday at Lake Como using as aids to drawing a camera obscura, a device which had been in use since the 16th Century by artists, including Vermeer, Joshua Reynolds, Thomas Sandby and Allan Ramsay, and a camera lucida, a prismatic device patented in 1806. His findings were read to the Royal Society in January 1839, just after Daguerre had announced his process in Paris. Talbot's "photogenic drawings" soon faded and he was filled with gloom as it appeared that Daguerre was well ahead of him. But his friend Sir John Herschel, a brilliant inventor with a European reputation, came to his rescue and renewed his optimism. It was Herschel who thought up the name photography to replace "photogenic drawing", besides coining the terms positive and negative and even the term snapshot.

A year later Talbot made the crucial discovery of the negative/positive photographic process which could produce multiple prints and which became the basis of all photography throughout the world until the arrival of digital cameras. He had discovered that paper treated with a subtractum of silver iodide and washed in gallic acid in conjunction with silver nitrate and acetic acid would produce a highly sensitive negative. On 23 September 1840 he had the dramatic experience of watching a picture gradually appearing in place of the invisible latent image caused by brief exposure to sunlight on a blank sheet of paper. This new process he called the Calotype.

Grove was fascinated by these techniques and their relative strengths and weaknesses. He soon got to know Talbot and they corresponded on scientific matters, and the re-organisation of the Royal Society. Talbot, who had a miserable experience of the vagaries of the law after a protracted and unsuccessful patents lawsuit in 1854, also corresponded with Grove and appears to have received some informal advice on patent law issues. Talbot in turn advised Grove about subjects and methods for photographic experiments. Grove's appreciation of Talbot's scientific standing is reflected in his efforts to persuade him, in 1868 to become President of the British Association for the Advancement of Science, an honour which Talbot declined due to the health of some members of his family and his spending time abroad.

In his inaugural lecture on 19 January 1842, the year in which he announced the discovery of the fuel cell, Grove wrote that he would not "dwell upon the beautiful recent application of artificial light....." but would "confine myself to a short exposé of the most remarkable discovery of modern times - the art of photography."

He began by describing how some substances, notable the salts of silver, decomposed when exposed to light and he instanced the process by which chloride of silver could be used to create a picture with reversed lights and shadows which could be fixed by being immersed in a solution of iodide of potassium. "This" he wrote "was the first and simple process of Mr. Talbot; but it is defective in many points. First, it is not sufficiently sensitive, requiring a strong light and a long time to produce an image: secondly, the lights and shadows are reversed: thirdly, the coarse structure of the finest paper does not admit of the delicate traces of objects being distinctly impressed." But, he said, "in the photographs of M. Daguerre, with which you are all familiar, the above defects are remedied...while Daguerre's process has been thus perfected, Mr. Talbot has much improved the photographic process on paper; and by his new method which he calls Calotype, portraits may be taken which, if they have not the minute perfection of the Daguerrotypes, have yet many practical advantages from the nature of the material used." Grove saw the superior perfection of the Daguerrotype in skilled hands but he did not realise that it was to be Talbot's process that would bring photography to the whole world. He admitted, however, that "It would be vain to attempt specifically to predict what may be the effect of Photography on future generations." He realised clearly enough the vast possibilities of this new invention, but he could not forsee how and in what form photography would develop. Two years later Grove wrote a short note for the British Association for the Advancement of Science, and this ran as follows –

"Mr Grove communicated experiments he had made with some success in obtaining a paper capable of giving positive photographs by one process, and avoiding the necessity of transfer, by which the imperfections of the paper are shown. As light favours many chemical actions, Mr Grove thought that a paper darkened by the sun (which darkening is supposed to result from the precipitation of silver) might be bleached by using a solvent which would not attack the silver in the dark, but would do so in the light. Among other acids tried, nitric acid succeeded best. Thus a darkened calotype paper is re-iodized by iodide of potassium, and then drawn over dilute nitric acid, one part acid to two and a half water; when so prepared it is rapidly bleached by exposure to light, and perfectly fixed by washing in water and dipping in hydrosulphite of soda, or bromide of potassium. If the acid be strong, say one-half water, the paper will be bleached in ten seconds by the sun, but then it bleaches in the dark.

Mr Grove showed some lithographs copied by this process; but stated that in the very few trials he had made with the camera the images had not been clear; that he had then tried the following method: - Let an ordinary calotype image or portrait be taken in a camera and developed by gallic acid, then drawn over iodide of potassium and nitric acid, and exposed to full sunshine; while bleaching the dark parts, the light is re-darkening the newly precipitated iodide in the lighter portions, and thus the negative picture is converted into a positive one. It is, however, faint, and gallic acid will not develop it; possibly some other solutions, such as those of iron, may; but Mr Grove had not had time to try them. He believed from what he had observed that a great many cases would be found in which a negative picture might be changed from a positive one, and that in some of these very good positive effects would probably be obtained."

That same year the Scottish painter David Hill, who much admired the founders of the Free Church of Scotland, and the photographer Robert Adamson, visited York and took pictures at the meeting of the British Association for the Advancement of Science, including one of Grove. Hill and Adamson had been encouraged by Talbot and his Scottish friend Sir David Brewster, and their later series of 'Newhaven Calotypes' of *The Fishermen and Women of the Firth of Forth* became one of the first and most important photographic records of the life and work of a whole community. The painter Clarkson Stanfield is reported to have exclaimed that he would rather have a set of them than the finest Rembrandts he ever saw.

Grove's interest in photography remained principally in its scientific process and what that told him about light, rather than the artistic developments of the likes of Hill and Adamson. In his lecture on Antagonism, given on 20 April 1888 when he was 78 (included as Appendix 1 to this book), he returned to this aspect of photography –

"...photography carries us further, it shows us that light acts on matter chemically, that it is capable of decomposing or forcing asunder the constituents of chemical compounds, and is therefore a force met by resistance."

He went on to describe experiments with letters cut out of paper placed between polished squares of glass with tin-foil on the outside. Grove deeply appreciated the work of the pioneers of photography, but his principal interest was in the advancement of science rather than the application of a new art.

Sir William Robert Grove, photograph in 1844 by David Octavius Hill and Robert Adamson, taken at the British Association for the Advancement of Science meeting at Nottingham in 1844

Michael Faraday by Thomas Phillips

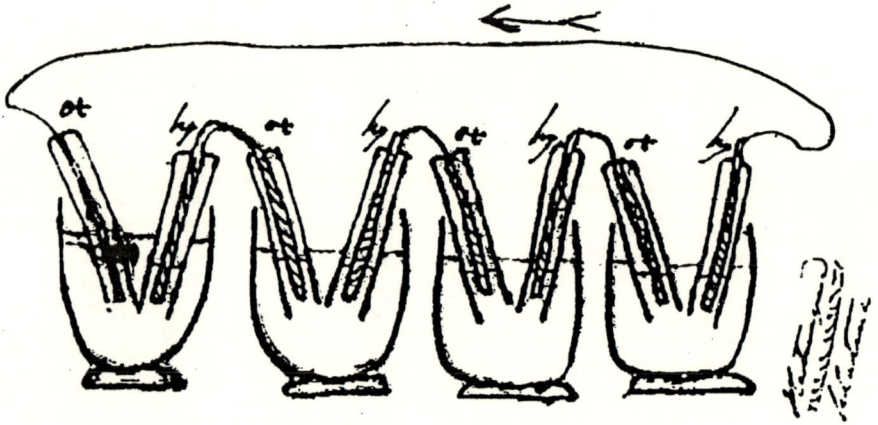

**Fuel cell sketch from Grove's letter to Faraday
22 October 1842,** Letter 1441 Faraday's published correspondence

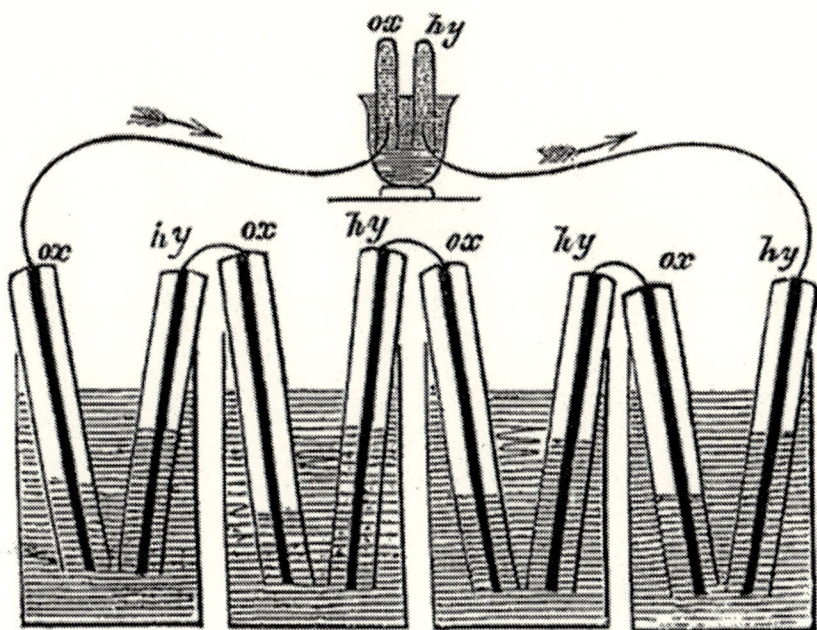

Grove's 1843 development of his fuel cell drawings
Philosophical Transactions 1843 – 'On the Gas Voltaic Battery –
Experiments made with a view of ascertaining the rationale of its action
and its application to Eudiometry'

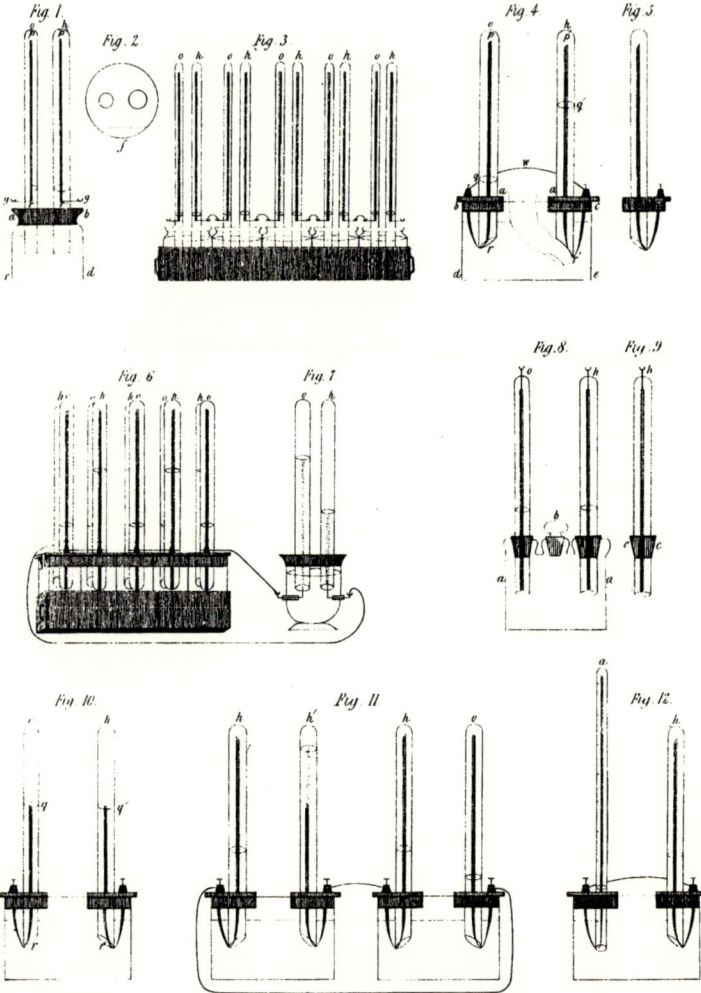

Grove's 1843 development of his fuel cell drawings
Philosophical Transactions 1843 – 'On the Gas Voltaic Battery –
Experiments made with a view of ascertaining the rationale of its action
and its application to Eudiometry'

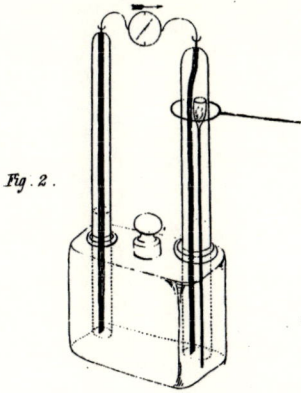
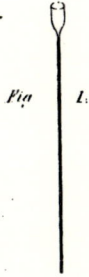
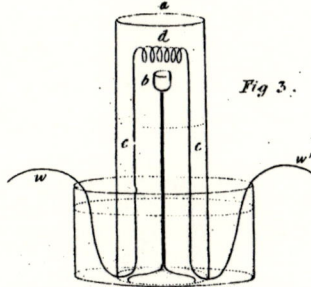

Phil Trans MDCCCXLV. Plate VI. p.352.

Fig. 2.

Fig. L.

Fig. 3.

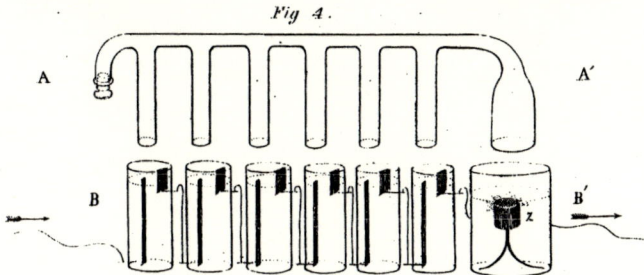

Fig 4.

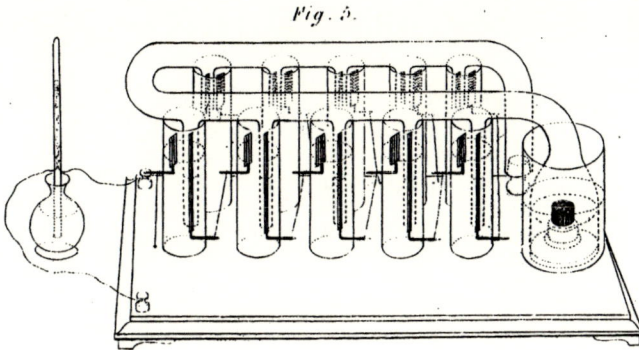

Fig. 5.

J. Basire. Lith.

Grove's 1845 drawings of the fuel cell apparatus
Philosophical Transactions 1845 – 'On the Gas Voltaic Battery –
Voltaic Action of Phosphorous, Sulphur and Hydrocarbons'

Lithograph of Grove by W. Bosley, after a Daguerrotype by Antoine Claudet, 21 February 1849

Mayall. Photo.

London & Brighton.

The Times

REPORT

OF THE

TRIAL OF WILLIAM PALMER,

FOR POISONING JOHN PARSONS COOK,

AT RUGELEY.

THE TALBOT ARMS, RUGELEY, THE SCENE OF COOK'S DEATH.

FROM THE SHORT-HAND NOTES TAKEN IN THE CENTRAL CRIMINAL COURT
FROM DAY TO DAY.

LONDON: WARD AND LOCK, 158, FLEET STREET.
1856.

61

Ὁ ἐναγὴς ἰατρὸς ἐξηγνίσθη ἐπὶ τῆς ἀγχόνης
τὴν 14 Ἰουνίου 1856 ἐν Σταφφὼρδ.

("The Accurst Surgeon," executed by the halter on June 14, 1856, in Stafford.)

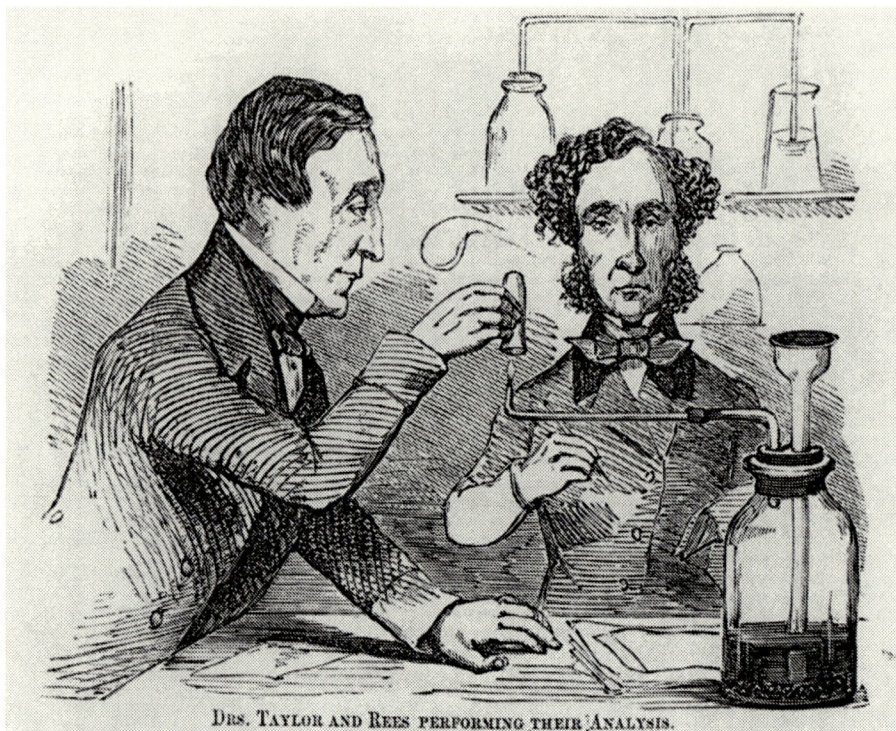

DRS. TAYLOR AND REES PERFORMING THEIR ANALYSIS.

"Drs Taylor and Rees performing their analysis" – from the 1856 Times Report of the Palmer Trial, a popular view of "sound science"

THE HON JUSTICE CROVE
COURT OF COMMON PLEAS

GROVE'S LEGAL CAREER

The Metropolitan Commission on Sewers of 1848 – 1849

Grove's Law Times obituary from 1896 records that he was appointed a member of the Metropolitan Commission on Sewers, which was set up in 1847 as part of a response to London's appalling health problems arising from its gross pollution.

In the first half of the 19th century, London's population was doubling, and the City was spreading rapidly outwards. Sanitation was primitive and had not kept pace. As more houses were built, many with the newly invented flushing water closet lavatories, and populations grew, the pressure on cesspits increased, and more sewerage was discharged to the rivers. The tributaries to the river Thames, with names like the Fleet, the West Bourne, the Holbourne and others disappeared beneath the advancing buildings, to be commemorated only in street names, and becoming little more than open sewers.

Typhoid fever was common, and cholera epidemics broke out in 1832. The Poor Law Commission, led by Edwin Chadwick, published a *Report on the Sanitary Condition of the Labouring Population of Great Britain* in 1842 and contaminated drinking water was identified as the main cause of disease, much as it is in many Third World countries today. It is said that the new Metropolitan Commission on Sewers ordered the closure of many cesspits, but this had the disastrous result of massive discharges of untreated sewerage into the rivers, and particularly the Thames. Further cholera outbreaks are said to have killed as many as 54,000 in 1848-49, and 31,000 in 1853-54. A better choice was the appointment of the great Victorian civil engineer Joseph Bazalgette by the Metropolitan Commission, as its chief engineer.

In 1858, the abysmal pollution of the river Thames resulted in what was known as 'the great stink' when a hot summer produced such awful smells through the city that disinfected curtains had to be hung across the windows of the House of Commons. This seems to have prompted the Disraeli government into action, and further legislation was passed enabling Joseph Bazalgette to begin the construction of over 83 miles of huge intercepting sewers under London that gradually rendered it habitable once again.

The 1840s must in some ways have seemed an apocalyptic time, with the Irish potato blight and famine, and terrible outbreaks of typhoid, cholera and influenza killing thousands. But it was also a decade where Victorian society can be seen as feeling its way slowly towards a better state of society, with reformers like the great Earl of Shaftesbury and others returning time after time to efforts to improve factory conditions for women and children, to restrict the use of children as chimney sweeps, to reform the hours and conditions of their labour in the mines, and to introduce amendments to the poor laws and to set up the ragged schools. In some ways it was a decade when English society seemed to be trying to re-balance the wealth and comforts enjoyed by some and the squalor endured by many more.

Grove's Legal Practice

Most of Grove's working life at the Bar was spent in the practice of patent law, where his scientific and technical understanding must have been of great assistance to him. But he seems to have retained a healthy scepticism about the value of the branch of law in which he made his living, and interestingly, to have seen it very much from the viewpoint of a scientist.

Writing in *Blackwood's Magazine* in 1843, he doubted that patent law worked to the benefit of either science, or those seeking patents. He argued that most patents lodged at the Patent Office in Chancery Lane only benefited the revenue. It could take as long as fourteen years (the statutory limit of patent grants) to get manufacturers used to making the new product, and to introduce its value and uses to the public. This seems a curious observation given the usual clichés about Victorian Britain being a hotbed of new inventions. He noted that with the costs of lodging the patent being so high, even without its being contested in litigation, really useful scientific patents tended to fall by the wayside, while non-essential trivia such as "a patent ink-stand, a boot-heel, a shaving case or a button" stood a better chance of successful commercial development.

Instead, Grove argued that …"we seriously incline to think that, as the matter at present stands, an entire erasure from the statute-books of patent provision would be of service to science, and perhaps to the community; each tradesman would depend for success upon his own activity, and the perfection he could give his manufacture, and the scientific searcher after experimental truths would not find his path barred by prohibitions from speculative empires." He gave the instance of the controversial patent granted to Daguerre, as the Daguerrotype forerunner of photography, and questioned the benefit of allowing such a wide area of scientific inquiry being foreclosed for fourteen years, which he thought of more consequence than the injury to any individual by losing out on royalties for the use of the patent. By comparison, he granted that Mr Talbot was perfectly entitled to patent his Calotype process of early photography, but that the Royal Society should not then have given him a medal for it.

Grove showed a somewhat Olympian disdain for the tendency to make money out of scientific invention, declaring that ..."If parties look to money as their reward, they have no right to look for fame; to those who sell the produce of their brains, the public owes no debt.". Before he came to be a dominant figure in patent law litigation, however, Grove's fame as a scientist led him to be instructed as part of the legal defence team on one of the most notorious murder cases of the Victorian age.

The trial of William Palmer, the "Rugeley poisoner"

Grove's correspondence, and some of that from his friends and contemporaries, might suggest that science was his first interest, while the pursuit of his legal career was something he had to do to support his large family. While there may have been some truth in this, at least some of the legal cases in which he was involved were among the most sensational of their day, and none more so that that of the "Rugeley poisoner" William Palmer.

Palmer's trial for the murder by poisoning of his friend John Cook has been described as "one of the greatest trials in the history of English law", and Grove was the second defence counsel. The trial is meticulously recorded in the *Notable British Trials* series, edited by George Knott, Eric Watson and James Hodge, which is highly recommended to students of the genre. Apart from the Victorian Gothic facts of the case itself, it attracted the participation of the most brilliant lawyers of its day.

67

Background

Dr William Palmer of Rugeley in Staffordshire was 31 at the time of his trial for murder in 1855. He had practised medicine, after a fashion, until two or three years before, but appears to have given it up to pursue his interests in horse racing and betting.

Palmer's murky background was not fully revealed at the trial itself. It appears that he began life as an indentured druggist, but this came to an end when he was suspected of stealing money from customers. He was apprenticed as a surgeon, but left under a cloud, with suspicions of affairs with women and irregularities with money. He briefly attended the Staffordshire Infirmary as a "walking pupil", and then, despite his past, trained at St Bartholomew's ('Barts') hospital in London as a surgeon, and returned to Rugeley to practice as a doctor. In 1847 he married Annie Brooks, a Chancery ward and illegitimate daughter of a Colonel Brooks.

At the time of his trial, Palmer was in correspondence with a woman in Staffordshire who had letters from Palmer apparently referring to an illegal abortion. He sent her some money in an effort to get them back. He appears to have had an illegitimate child by another Rugeley woman, and the child visited him after his marriage, and then died.

Palmer's mother-in-law came to live with him and his wife, but died within a fortnight. In 1850 a Mr Bladon, to whom Palmer owed £800 for horse racing bets, came to stay with Palmer, and died, in circumstances quite similar to those which became the subject of his trial for the murder of Cook in 1855 – a hasty burial was arranged.

In 1854 Palmer insured his wife's life for £13,000, and six months later she died, again in circumstances very similar to those of Cook. Palmer's friend Dr Bamford, aged eighty two, was induced to certify death. The way in which Palmer used the money from his wife's insurance policy to finance the merry-go-round of his most pressing racing debts featured largely at his trial. In personal terms he appears to have been consolable, as exactly nine months after his wife's death, the maid in their household bore him another illegitimate child.

Palmer then set about insuring the life of his brother Walter for a further £13,000, and very shortly after that Walter died. The policy had been lodged by Palmer with one of his racing moneylenders, Pratt, in order to secure advances against it. By this stage, however, the insurance company was becoming suspicious, and its refusal to pay out on the policy led to acute financial problems for Palmer, and may have contributed to the circumstances of the death of John Cook.

In 1855 Palmer was still trying to effect life insurances, this time on the life of a stable lad called Bates, in the improbable sums of £25,000 and £10,000, urged on by Palmer's racing crony and subsequent victim John Cook, who assured Bates, "You had better do it; it will be for your benefit, and you'll be quite safe with Palmer." Cook was to die in agonies, the prosecution said from poisoning at Palmer's hand later that year. Indictments were being prepared against Palmer for the murder of both his wife and his brother, but these were not proceeded with after the verdict in the first trial. Bates the stable lad may be thought to have had a lucky escape: the life expectancy of the subjects of Palmer's insurance policies was not great.

Counsel and Judges

The Palmer trial was so notorious in its day that three judges were brought in to preside over it, with Lord Chief Justice Campbell, Mr Justice Cresswell and Mr Baron Alderson.

Local prejudice and feeling against Palmer were running so high in Staffordshire by the time of the trial that it was feared that there could be no prospect of his receiving a fair trial there. So a separate Act of Parliament, *Act 19 Vict cap 16*, was passed specially to allow the trial to be held in London.

The prosecution was led by the Attorney General Sir Alexander Cockburn, who later became Lord Chief Justice. Cockburn is credited with having helped Palmerston with some of his most famous speeches, and with making his own brilliant debating replies to Gladstone in the House of Commons. He is supposed to have been one of the most formidable advocates and devastating cross-examiners of his day, and the authors of the *Notable Trials* volume speak with awe of the way in which his cross-examination destroyed the credibility of the key defence witness at the Palmer trial, the shady attorney and financial associate of Palmer, Jeremiah Smith. The Attorney General is credited with having made his entire closing speech in the trial, page after page of detailed commentary on all the evidence, without reference to a single note.

Edwin James Q.C., who also appeared for the prosecution, was another brilliant advocate, but was later disbarred for financial irregularities, and went on the stage at the Winter Garden Theatre in New York. Evidently Grove's legal career was not exclusively made up of a dusty collection of patent cases. Three other Counsel appeared for the prosecution.

Mr Serjeant Shee led the defence team for William Palmer. Sir William Shee, who was aged 52 at the time of the trial, had been a strong advocate of Catholic Emancipation in Parliament, and went on to become the first Roman Catholic judge since the Reformation when he was appointed to the High Court bench. At and after the Palmer trial, Shee, who had not defended in a murder trial before, was strongly criticised for having made a trenchant statement of his own belief in Palmer's innocence ...“I commence his defence, I say it in all sincerity, with an entire conviction of his innocence....”. He was also much criticised for referring so extensively in his speech to Palmer's family life, when the jury may have heard about the strong suspicions that he had murdered his wife.

Grove himself was the second defence Counsel. The *Notable Trials* volume describes him as ...“in one respect the most distinguished of all the persons who took part in the trial...”, adding “it is sufficient to say that he had published in 1846 the great book “the Correlation of Physical Forces”, which placed him in the front rank of European science.” The commentary notes that ...“It was probably his scientific eminence that led to his brief in the Palmer case...,” which makes sense, given the detailed examination and cross examination of the scientific and medical witnesses, especially on the after-effects of strychnia poisoning, and whether if strychnia had been used, traces should have been discovered by the post mortem.

The third of the four defence Counsel, Edward Vaughan Hyde Kennealy, was another highly colourful character, a poet and writer as well as an advocate, who went on to represent the Tichborne Claimant. His ferocious attacks on the Chief Justice in a paper which he edited eventually led to his being disbarred.

The death of Cook

John Cook was 28 at the time of his death. He had been articled as a solicitor, but, like Palmer, seems to have given up his attempts to join a profession in order to spend his time betting and following horse racing. He fell in with Palmer and seems to have gone to races and lived in betting circles in his company.

By the time of the murder, Palmer's finances were in a parlous state, and his creditors and moneylenders were pressing hard. The insurance company was refusing to pay out on the insurance policy on his brother Walter's life, and the money lender to whom this policy had been pledged was threatening to close in and to sue Palmer and his mother, which would have been awkward, as Palmer appears to have forged his mother's signature on a discounted bill, and she could have faced legal proceedings as well.

On 13 November 1855 Cook's horse "Polestar" won a race and £2,500 at Shrewsbury, and Cook and Palmer repaired to the Raven Hotel in that town. Cook became violently ill, and Palmer attended to him, taking him drinks. Cook was apparently in fairly delicate health and there is some suggestion that he may have had syphilis. The defence tried to establish at the trial that Cook's own health was an issue.

On 15 November Cook and Palmer returned to the Talbot Arms in Rugeley. Palmer took Cook some coffee, after which Cook became very ill again. Palmer ordered a bowl of broth for Cook, and handed it to a maid saying that a friend had sent it. She tried a spoonful before handing it to Cook, and herself became very ill. Palmer called in his octogenaran doctor friend, Dr Bamford to attend to Cook, and meanwhile himself went to Tattersalls in London where he gave instructions to Tattersalls agents about the disposal of Cook's winnings, taking the opportunity to settle the most pressing of his own bills.

While Palmer was away, Cook had no more symptoms. When Palmer returned to his bedside, Cook became much worse. There were violent screams from his bedroom at midnight.

Palmer meanwhile dropped in to a local chemist to purchase some strychnia, and when seen by an acquaintance took care to draw him away. Quite why a non-practising doctor needed 6 grains of strychnia, some prussic acid and some Batley's solution of opium was never satisfactorily explained. The circumstantial evidence in the case, and Palmer's own behaviour, must have given his defence Counsel a mountain to climb in preparing his defence.

Meanwhile Palmer tried to get the postmaster at Rugeley to fill out a cheque for £350 in his favour, saying that his poor friend Cook was too ill to draw it. The prosecution said that Palmer forged Cook's signature upon it.

The luckless Cook declared that "Palmer, I will have no more medicine tonight, no more pills". But Palmer had other ideas. He got Dr Bamford to write directions on a further box of pills, drew another witness's attention to Dr Bamford's writing, and then at 10.30 p.m. pressed Cook to take his further medicine. By 12.15 p.m. Cook was screaming "For God's sake get the doctor, I am going to be ill as I was last night", and later that night he died.

By 22 November, Palmer was trying to pass off another £4,000 of bills as negotiated for Cook's benefit, but even the Rugeley postmaster refused to sign anything further, declaring "Good God! The man is dead!".

Cook's stepfather Mr Stevens appeared at Rugeley, and became sufficiently suspicious about the circumstances of Cook's death that he arranged for a post mortem examination to be carried out. Even then, Palmer seems to have behaved extremely suspiciously, finding his way into the room where the post mortem on his own victim was being performed, handling jars containing various organs which later proved to have their seals broken, and apparently offering the lad charged with taking them to the station to send to the laboratory £10 to have the fly coach overturned and the sample jars broken. Macabre details of this kind in trial reports appear to have preceded television, films and other forms of entertainment for the neo-Gothic tastes of Victorian England.

Even after an inquest was convened, Palmer seems to have done his defence no favours by writing to the coroner, and mistakenly offering him gifts of game. Not surprisingly he was charged with Cook's murder and sent for trial.

The medical evidence - William Grove Q.C. in action

As Victorian murder trials were life or death affairs, it is not surprising that this was a highly charged trial with much at stake. There is no record of Grove being swept along by Shee's emphatic statement of his belief in Palmer's innocence, or Kennealy's later angry denunciation of the Lord Chief Justice for bias in favour of the prosecution. But the meticulous verbatim records of the *Notable Trials* volume gives a rare account of Grove in action as a barrister, dealing principally with the examination in chief and cross examination of the leading medical witnesses, but also being entrusted with the cross-examination of some of the other prosecution witnesses.

Charles Newton gave evidence for the prosecution about Palmer's purchase of strychnia on 19 November. "Cross-examined by Mr Grove" he admitted that "The first time I informed the Crown with reference to the purchase of the 3 grains on the Monday was on Tuesday last". Grove was therefore trying to establish that this witness had recently added to his evidence. The Attorney General picked up the point in re-examination, with the witness explaining that he had not mentioned it before because his employer was not on speaking terms with Palmer and he thought his employer would be angry.

Henry Daniel, a surgeon of the Bristol Hospital was called by the prosecution to give evidence about tetanus, asserting that he never knew it to be brought on by syphilis. Grove's cross-examination prompted him to admit that "I have been out of practice some

73

seventeen or eighteen months, and have not looked into the reported cases of tetanus of late."

Professor Robert Christison FRCP from Edinburgh University was called by the Crown to give evidence about the effects of strychnia poisoning, and its observed effects on various animals. Grove led the cross examination of this important witness by detailed reference to the witness's own book. This was very careful work, with Grove asking questions leading to the important point about whether or not traces of strychnia should be expected to be present after death, if resinous substances were used in a pill –
"The strychnia would be discharged with them would it not? – Certainly, or gradually acted upon with the resinous substances.
I suppose if the resinous substances prevented the poison acting rapidly, it would prevent its absorption into the blood? – For a time.
If so, the more likely to leave portions of it in the stomach or intestines as the case may be? – The more likely."
Once again, the Attorney General carried out the re-examination, which might suggest that the prosecution was fully aware of the potential significance of Grove's line of questioning and its possible effects.

When the defence later called its own evidence, Grove led the examination in chief of the most important of the medical and scientific witnesses.

Professor Thomas Nunneley FCS from the Leeds School of Medicine was taken through his evidence by Grove, declaring that in his opinion Cook died from some convulsive disease. Grove must have asked him what he based that opinion on, because when he said that it was founded in part on the evidence before the Court, there was a flurry of interventions from the Lord Chief Justice and other members of the bench about what could or could not be properly concluded from the evidence of Cook's health or his possible syphilis. Apart from general evidence to the effect that Cook's actions were not consistent with some of the observed effects of strychnia poisoning with which he was familiar, this witness was used by Grove to bring out the important evidence that if strychnia had been present, he would certainly have expected to be able to find traces of it after the post mortem examination, and one of the relatively few strong points in the defence

74

was that no such traces were found. Grove's examination in chief was clearly a very detailed and lengthy undertaking, covering various experiments with strychnia upon cats, and the observed post mortem effects on humans. He seems to have been quite at home with the scientific detail when examining this witness. The Attorney General's cross examination, aimed at picking holes in the evidence which Grove had examined in chief, was twice as long.

Grove's next major witness was Professor William Herepath, Professor in Chemistry and Toxicology at the Bristol Medical School. Grove asked Herepath –

"Are you of opinion, as a chemist, that where strychnia has been taken in a sufficient dose to poison, it can be detected, and ought to be detected? – Yes, up to the time the body is decomposed completely…I am of the opinion that strychnia ought to have been detected if it had existed in the jar containing the stomach, even in the state it was.".

Herepath was cross-examined by the Attorney General, but Grove re-examined, and Herepath stated that he had dissolved the tenth part of a grain of strychnia in a gallon of water (1 in 70,000) and that he was still able to demonstrate the presence of strychnia in the tenth of one drop of water.

Grove went on to take other defence witnesses through the medical evidence, which was really the main plank in the defence case. He handled the examination in chief of John Ross, a surgeon from the London Hospital, about the symptoms of tetanus in a patient there. He took Professor Richard Partridge, Professor of Anatomy at King's College London, through his evidence on the types of tetanic convulsions. And he was entrusted with the examination in chief of a saddler from Rugeley, George Myatt, who had been staying near Palmer and Cook.

The defence were not permitted a closing speech, and the Attorney General made his formidable summary for the prosecution before the Lord Chief Justice began his summary for the jury. Page after page of the Attorney General's speech was devoted to the medical evidence with which Grove had been chiefly concerned, and if anything could have saved Palmer from the gallows, it must have been the unexplained fact that no traces of strychnia were found by the post mortem examination when the prosecution maintained that Palmer had caused the death of Cook by administering strychnia. Palmer himself made a deeply ambiguous declaration that he was "innocent of poisoning Cook by strychnia", which must have left many wondering what else he might have used.

But in the end, Palmer was overwhelmed by the weight of circumstantial evidence, his clear motives, his past actions, and his financial transactions profiting from the death The jury convicted him, and the Lord Chief Justice sentenced Palmer to death by hanging, the sentence to be carried out in Stafford. On the day of his execution, some 20,000 to 30,000 people turned out to jeer and hiss at the condemned man, so great was the public outcry against him. And after his execution, his remaining stable was broken up and sold, and it is curious to note that Prince Albert bought his horse Trickstress for 230 guineas. Grove had played a notable and spirited part in the unsuccessful defence of one of the most notorious criminals of the Victorian age.

Grove's patent law practice

Hills v London Gas Light Co 1860

Hills v The London Gas Light Company was a patent case from 1860 that concerned the processes for cleaning the gas that went into the gaslights of Victorian London. Hills claimed that he had an "improved mode of manufacturing gas", reflected in his patents. The disputes in the case concerned whether he had invented all the processes described, or relied in part on the inventions described by others, and whether the claimant to the patented process had described it accurately enough in supporting documents to prevent others from claiming it as their own.

The earliest patents at issue had been filed only three years after Queen Victoria came to the throne. The science described, bubbling sulphuretted hydrogen through sawdust or compressed peat, has a period ring, and suggests one of many reasons why London's air in Victorian Times would have been affected by such institutions as the

Gas Light and Coke Company of Westminster and the Chartered Gas Company of Brick Lane. There is a passing mention of gas companies being permitted to discharge their refuse into the river, which cannot have helped with pollution of the river Thames. In a much later case when he was a judge in 1877, Grove made rulings against the public nuisance caused by this kind of pollution, where the St Helens Chemical Company was discharging foul smelling pollution into the sewers. That company had the misfortune to have its case heard by a judge who knew exactly what sulphuretted hydrogen smelled like, and who had served on the Metropolitan Commission on Sewers.

Grove was one of five Counsel, including the Attorney General, on one side of the patents arguments in the *Hills* case, with another four Counsel on the other side, and senior judges presiding. Victorian litigation was not a lean operation. It appears that Grove's arguments about the nature of "oxides" and the way in which they were described in the various patent depositions and pleadings were fairly decisive in leading the court to conclude that the original patent should be allowed to stand.

Royal Commission on the Patent Laws 1862

The Royal Commission on the Patent Laws of 1862 was set up to look at ways of streamlining a system which had, since the passage of amending legislation in 1852, led to "protracted litigation and consequent expense", amounting to joint legal costs in two of the cases cited before the Commission of £26,000 and £15,000 respectively, vast sums in today's money. It also considered issues such as the difficulties encountered by the War Department from the multitude of patents taken out for inventions in use by the naval and military departments. It made recommendations for resolution of cases on written evidence alone, and recommended that patent law cases be heard by a judge sitting with expert assessors rather than a jury – very similar arguments are heard today about the way in which complex fraud cases should be heard and decided.

Grove participated in the work of the Commission as a Commissioner, and also submitted a learned memorandum with an *Analysis of and Observations on the Law of France*, comparing patent law proceedings there. On 10th February 1863 he gave evidence as a witness, based on his estimated 20 years experience as a patent lawyer. He tended to favour maintaining reasonably high fees for obtaining patents, so as to oblige poor applicants to undergo the necessity of "getting a capitalist to take up the invention". He gave as a further reason for this the somewhat startling suggestion that -

> …"poor men are very frequently uneducated, and they are frequently sanguine, particularly if they are of the inventor class, and if they were induced by the cheapness of Patents to patent their inventions, not only should we have a very great increase in the number of Patents, but many of these men would be for five or six years, or possibly more, dancing after a foolish idea. I believe that none but those practically versed in the subject know how difficult it is to disabuse the mind of a supposed inventor of his invention. I have frequently shown men the thing which they have supposed themselves to have invented; they go away disappointed on seeing it, but the next day they come and say there is some distinction in their invention. They cannot give up the idea when it is once in their minds, and if you tempt them by too cheap a Patent, you do them a serious damage, you lead them away from their trade or occupation."

He explained that was not a matter of right, but was originally a statutory privilege, or a form of the monopoly originally conferred by the Crown. He thought that patents were originally designed to protect "substantial manufactures" such as great improvements in the manufacture of copper or iron, the introduction of aluminium, "the power loom, the Jacquard loom, the steam engine and other things of that sort". He deplored the more recent trend towards patenting …"a peculiar method for cutting the little puckered linen which is sewn and used for short frills, or a particular shape of the brim of a lady's hat…"

He saw the investigation of patents as carried out by the Law Officers as being of some value, particularly in discouraging dealers in patents and fraudulent patents taken out to catch up with someone else's invention. He recommended having people with real knowledge of mechanics and chemistry assisting the Law Officers in making their investigations.

Much has changed in the issues confronting patent lawyers today. Their practice is apt to be much more international, as they seek to defend or challenge the application of patents over a wider range of jurisdictions and markets. The time taken to be able to introduce patents to manufacturers has reduced drastically, with the capacity of emerging markets such as China to manufacture a huge range of products on demand for Western manufacturers as well as their own. The international observance of patents, or lack of it, are very much a live issue for many patent holders, trying to stem the tide of imitations and unlicensed 'pirated' versions of their products.

Some aspects of patent law would still be familiar to Grove. Some inventors are notoriously reluctant to allow anyone else to develop their inventions, preferring the trouble and expense of holding expensive patent rights to the uncertainty of sharing the spoils of their inventions with others better able to exploit them – rather as if they held a lottery ticket.

But what would Grove have made of the way in which pharmaceutical companies patent medicines worldwide, and have to be browbeaten into allowing generic versions of drugs to combat AIDS or malaria to be manufactured and marketed locally? And the counter argument that without proper protection from exploitation by others, pharmaceutical companies would never invest the huge sums necessary to prove new drugs and to bring them to the market? What would his attitude have been to the purported patenting of more and more aspects of human and animal DNA, or the way in which plant products from rainforests are worked on, patented in the West and then sold back to the indigenous peoples whose forests were explored to find the plant products in the first place? Or McDonalds' efforts to patent the way they make a sandwich? Would Grove have preferred to think that his computer software was contributing to the fiercely protected intellectual property of a Microsoft, or would he have opted instead for one of the freely available software systems operating outside the constraints of modern intellectual property law?

It may be thought that Grove would have instinctively aligned himself with whichever approach he thought most likely to lead to the free advancement of science and scientific knowledge, which may have interested him more than who stood to gain millions from their patents and intellectual property.

Young v Fernie 1864

The case of *Young v Fernie* of 1864 has been described as a classic Victorian patent case. It must have been one of Grove's most famous victories, and it shows him at the top of his form as an advocate, also bringing to bear all of his formidable scientific knowledge. It was a massive case, with Grove leading a team of no less than seven Counsel for the patentee Young against the Attorney General and five other Counsel for the defendant Fernie, with over 31 days of evidence and argument in the Chancery Court before the Vice Chancellor.

James Young had started his researches after leasing a petroleum spring in Derbyshire, and concluding that petroleum was the result of a natural distillation of bituminous substances by the heat of the earth, condensed through the sandstone formation. By 1850 he had letters patent issued in 1850 that gave him fourteen years of exclusive rights in England and the colonies to use his invention, which consisted of an improved way of heating and treating bituminous coal in order to extract paraffin oil. On this process, Young founded a major business, and he took out patents, which he defended vigorously and at considerable cost, in Scotland and elsewhere – the judgement refers to similar patents in Ireland and Scotland, and a big business built up to exploit them. Young had already successfully defended his patent in litigation before the Court of Session in Scotland. The paraffin oil was exhibited among the chemical contributions at the Great Exhibition in London in 1851. The reference to the patent rights extending to the colonies gives a clue as to how much was at stake, at a time when England's colonies were so extensive.

The patent specification described breaking down bituminous coals, parrot coal, cannel coal and gas coal, to pieces about the size of a hen's egg, placing them in a retort at about 55^0 Fahrenheit, and then gradually heating them up to 'a low red heat' to draw off the paraffin oil. Young

80

had found, and his patent reflected, a particular combination of processes and temperatures that produced these results. Those disputing his patent and claiming to be able to use similar processes argued that there was basically nothing new in this, that paraffin had been discovered before, in 1830 by Dr Reichenbach from beechwood tar, that it could be produced by similar means and so on. Grove's task, therefore, was to establish the originality and value of the particular combination of processes in Young's patent.

Grove argued that Young's patent specification described the very best mode of obtaining the products desired. A specification was an instruction to the present manufacturing world. He dismissed the argument that any previous reference to the terms of a patent that pre-dated it would invalidate it, citing the case in which he had played a part, *Hills v The London Gas Light Company* –

> "The mere fact of there being a previous publication in which the patentee's invention is jumbled up among other things does not invalidate the patent. In order to amount to an anticipation the discovery must have been previously disclosed, or in other words, it must be shown that the information contained in the specification must have been previously given to the public."

Then Grove went on to give an account of what it really meant to be an original inventor, and how useful inventions that result in patents are often the result of incremental change which then results in discovery of what is really useful –

> "The world, as it were, works up to a discovery, and between the successful discovery and the unsuccessful efforts there is frequently but a very small step. But, as a general rule, that portion of the public who are concerned in a particular branch of manufacture, be it chemical or be it mechanical, are the best judges of who has really hit the nail on the head, if it were permitted to use the expression. Therefore, when they recognise it the public gets possession of it, and their judgement is not commonly erroneous."

He dealt with attacks on the originality of patents (and scientific ideas) with similar clarity and energy –

> "But always when a discovery has been made, when the public has reaped the fruits of it, there is no case, and never was a case, either in the history of pure science or in the history of practical discovery, where it is not alleged, "If you look at such a book, and such another book, you will find that so and so has been done, and you will find that it has been anticipated." That is partly true and partly false. There are in all such cases approximate anticipations. The difference is that one man gets at the points, hits upon the real thing that will do it, and the reason why it will, whereas other people, although they may have got the thing, have not acquired an accurate knowledge which will enable them with certainty to produce it."

We have seen how in *The Birth of the Fuel Cell 1835-1845*, Dr Ulf Bossel explains how Schoenbein in 1838 discovered the fuel cell effect, while it was Grove who went on to discover and demonstrate the actual fuel cell in operation. In 1866, in his Presidential Address to the British Association for the Advancement of Science, Grove was to take as his theme 'continuity', and the way in which knowledge was a continuous process, reached by small steps. In the courtroom in *Young v Fernie* in 1864, Grove deployed these ideas about the progressive originality of invention as a formidably well-informed advocate –

> "The common clap-trap notion of the invention of gunpowder is this: that a monk of Cologne named Schwarz put sulphur, charcoal, and saltpetre into a pot, and then when he melted them altogether it exploded and blew off the top of the pot…whereas it was well known that gunpowder was originally a Chinese invention, and that it got from China to Arabia, Arabia to Greece, and from Greece to England."

After describing the use of gunpowder as "Greek fire" at the Battle of Crécy, and the way in which public understanding of its usefulness and how to make it evolved, Grove returned to his theme of invention –

..."the great discoverer is the man who gives the world a clear power of repetition – a clear mode of reproducing the result which he says he has arrived at. That man is the discoverer...It is very easy to say that such a thing existed in A's patent or B's patent, because we now know the conditions, and know the temperature of heat necessary to produce this and that effect, and we can apply the value of the new chemical discovery of paraffine to commercial uses, as applied by Mr Young. But at these antecedent periods, they did not know this, and the proof that they did not know it was that in the year 1850 paraffine oil was an unknown and an undiscovered substance."

Grove went on to give the court a bit of a tutorial in chemistry, in clear, lively and understandable terms. He was in command of his brief, and showing every sign of enjoying himself. The plaintiff, his client, he concluded, had made an important practical discovery, which was protected by his patent. It was equally clear that the defendants had infringed the patent, and the plaintiff was entitled to the judgment of the court.

In reply, the Attorney General and his team of five other Counsel called witness after witness and cited case after case in their efforts to show that paraffin could be produced in other ways, and that Young's discovery was not new. They appear to have bombarded the court with legal precedent, in a workmanlike but somewhat pedestrian forensic performance. The Attorney General on the subject of the "low red heat" required to generate paraffin oil was by no means as convincing as Grove.

Grove was equally confident when he came to reply to the Attorney General's case. The fallacy in the defendant's argument, he said coolly, lay in applying subsequent knowledge to an anterior state of facts –

"One man might anticipate in general terms what a subsequent observer reduced to a definite practical form which ensured reproduction. Leland undoubtedly saw the planet Neptune centuries before, but that did not detract from the credit due to Le Verrier and Galle. The discoverer who first gave definite

83

information sufficient to ensure reproduction was able to support a patent for discovery."

His demolition of the defendant's case was masterly and authoritative. In giving judgment for the plaintiff, the Vice Chancellor adopted and accepted many of Grove's arguments. He noted that several witnesses for the defendants had been engaged in "laboriously endeavouring" to make the discovery that Young made, with very little success. They did not discover that cannel and other coals which yield olefiant and other highly illuminating gases were the proper material. It did not help the defendant's case that one such witness had tried to submit oils to the Great Exhibition of 1851, but that they were rejected and refused a place "on account of their objectionable quality and offensive smell." The judge doubted the relevance of many of the cases cited before him, and was unimpressed by the quality of some of the witnesses, particular scientific witnesses who appeared to have varied their evidence from earlier patent litigation on the same patent. The Vice Chancellor noted a description of paraffin in 1854 as something that had never got beyond the laboratory, and he concluded that –

> "What the law looks to is the inventor and discoverer who finds out and introduces a manufacture which supplies the market for useful and commercial purposes with an article which was previously little more than the ornament of a museum."

With this in mind, and the fact that the same patent had already been successfully defended before the Lord Chief Justice of England and an English jury and the Lord President of the Court of Session and a Scots jury, the Vice Chancellor gave judgement on all issues to the plaintiffs, an outstanding result for Grove and his clients. With hindsight, it is somewhat ironic that this forensic victory should have been achieved by the inventor of the fuel cell in defence of a patent for the handling of fossil fuels.

Jordan and Another v Moore

In the case of *Jordan v Moore* in 1866, Grove was unable to persuade the court that his plaintiff client's inventions were the proper subject of a patent. The facts were a further example of the way in which patent cases closely reflected the progress of the Industrial Revolution in

Victorian Britain. Jordan's claim concerned his use and development of an improved iron frame for building ships, to be covered by timber cladding. Grove's suggestion that his client's 'complete iron frame or skeleton, with a covering or skin of timber' was "a combination never before suggested in ship building" could not be fully maintained. The court held that the combination of iron and timber in the construction of ships was already well known and commonly used, and that as a result the patent could not be sustained.

Henderson v The Mostyn Copper Company Limited

Henderson v The Mostyn Copper Company Limited in 1868 was a complex matter where the defendants suspended royalty payment to the plaintiff patent holder, alleging that he had not done enough under a covenant between them to prevent the Runcorn Alkali Company from infringing the patent, which was for methods of concentrating and extracting metals from ores. Royalties payments due were for £2 10 shillings per ton of fine copper. Grove was part of a legal team that managed to show that the defendants were not justified in suspending their royalty payments.

Bovill and Another v Finch

The case of *Bovill and Another v Finch* in 1870 saw Grove acting for a patent holder who had invented improved methods of manufacturing meal and flour from wheat and grain, registering patents in England, Scotland and Ireland. The case turned on Victorian patent legislation and its different effect in different jurisdictions. The Scots patent was held to be void, but Grove managed to argue successfully that the others could be prolonged. This is one of the last records of Grove in action as a Queen's Counsel, as in 1871 he was made a Judge of the Common Pleas, and began a third career of 16 years on the High Court Bench.

Grove's judicial career

Grove was appointed as a High Court judge in the Court of Common Pleas in November 1871. His Law Times obituary many years later in 1896 remarked –

"It was thought that the new Judge would be especially valuable in the trial of patent cases, but in our system there is no classification of courts which secures that patent actions shall be tried before judges who know something of scientific subjects, and Mr Justice Grove shared the general business of the Courts with the other judges and a patent action rarely fell to his lot. It is idle therefore to discuss whether he did well or ill, that particular class of work. In this work he showed a perfectly competent knowledge of law, was patient and courteous; whilst we cannot select any judgement of his, of the nature which makes a judicial reputation, there are plenty which prove him to be a sound and careful lawyer. And if questions of science cropped up, he did not use his superior knowledge to nonplus those engaged but only to help the discovery of truth."

It is right to say that the Victorian courts which provided Grove with interesting and rewarding second and third careers, as counsel and judge, were regarded by others as a nightmare. In folio parts between 1852 and 1853 Dickens published *Bleak House*, and his withering scorn in the famous opening chapter for the workings of the Chancery court, as exemplified by the endless suit in *Jarndyce v Jarndyce*, can still make lawyers hang their heads (for a while, at any rate) today –

"And hard by Temple Bar, in Lincoln's Inn Hall, at the very heart of the fog, sits the Lord High Chancellor in his High Court of Chancery.
Never can there come fog too thick, never can there come mud and mire too deep, to assort with the groping and floundering condition which this High Court of Chancery, most pestilent of hoary sinners, holds, this day, in the sight of heaven and earth….

…The Chancellor is about to bow to the bar, when the prisoner is presented. Nothing can possibly come of the prisoner's conglomeration, but his being sent back to prison; which is soon done. The man from Shropshire ventures another remonstrative "My lord!" but the Chancellor, being aware of him, has dextrously vanished. Everybody else vanishes too. A battery of blue bags is loaded with heavy charges of papers and carried off by clerks; the little mad old woman marches off with her documents; the empty court is locked up. If all the injustice it has committed, and all the misery it has caused, could only be locked up with it, and the whole burnt away in a great funeral pyre, - why, so much the better for other parties than the parties in Jarndyce and Jarndyce!"

All contemporary accounts appear to confirm that Grove as a judge was unfailingly courteous and helpful. But it is a fact that he was part of a system in grave need of reform. His finest original work may have been done in the scientific laboratories, and his reforming zeal expended upon the Royal Society, and the efforts to make it a place for more dedicated scientists rather than a haven for the interested amateur. At any rate, there is no evidence to suggest that by the time he became a High Court judge, Grove had the energy or zeal for reform from which the court system would have benefited. He had done his main work in the field of science, and worked on Royal Commissions for the reform of patent law and for the reform of metropolitan sewers, but the courts of late Victorian England had a way to go before they too were pushed reluctantly towards the twentieth century.

The Queen v Keyn 1876, Grove J Dissenting

Ferdinand Keyn was the officer in command of a Prussian vessel, the Franconia, carrying the German mails from Hamburg to St Thomas in the west Indies. The Franconia had taken on an English pilot at Grimsby, but on the night of 17 February 1876, 1.9 miles S.S.E. from Dover and 2.5 miles from Dover beach, she ran down, struck and sunk the British steamer Strathclyde, on its way from London to Bombay. A passenger, Jessie Dorcas Young was drowned, and the Captain of the Franconia was arrested, and subsequently indicted, tried and convicted of manslaughter at the Central Criminal Court, under the jurisdiction of the Admiral of England.

The conviction was then challenged on the grounds that there was no jurisdiction in an English criminal court to try a foreign national for a criminal offence committed on a foreign ship on what were still regarded as the "high seas". The modern statements of what constitute a nation's "territorial waters" around its coasts had not then been firmly established in customary international law or by Treaty. The Crown argued that as the offence took place within three miles of the English coast, it was committed within the jurisdiction of the English courts.

The case was of fundamental importance to Britain's interests as a great maritime power. It must have been a touchy matter politically, as the proud nation states of the 19th century were loathe to have their citizens subjected to foreign laws and extra-territorial jurisdiction unless the facts fully justified it. Memories of the War of 1812 with America, which was partly precipitated by the Royal Navy's interception of American ships while enforcing the blockade of Napoleonic Europe, must have been fresh in 1876 when *Keyn* was decided. This case concerned a subject of Prussia, a growing military power in late 19th century Europe. But beyond that, the case does seem to have required the court to go back to first principles. What were a nation's rights to exert its jurisdiction over the waters immediately around its coasts?

By a narrow margin of 7 judges to 6, led by Lord Chief Justice Cockburn (the lead prosecutor of Palmer the poisoner in the case where Grove had been a senior defence counsel) the majority of the court held that there was no jurisdiction at the Central Criminal Court for the trial, and the manslaughter conviction was overturned. Grove was one of those entering a powerful dissenting judgement.

The style and standard of judicial argument in *Keyn* was learned, with a number of the judges breaking into lengthy quotations in Latin and French, and citing German, Italian and American authorities.

It was noted that the courts of the United States were already moving to claim and enforce their jurisdiction by a "marine league" around the coasts of America, and several leading American cases were cited, but apparently these claims were based upon legislation and Acts of Congress rather than common law and judicial interpretation. Lord Chief Justice Cockburn's leading judgement was really based around the need for, and absence of, clear legislation if a similar assertion of jurisdiction was to be applied here. It was for the legislature to address the issue, he argued, not the courts.

There was much discussion of the basis for the growing acceptance of states' rights to a "marine league" around their coasts, and the basis for that claim extending as far as a cannon could fire a cannon shot. One or two commentators pointed out dryly that if that were a proper basis for deciding jurisdiction, territorial claims would increase with improvements in artillery; and with modern missiles, many states would be able to claim each others' territory.

English legislation, particularly on Customs, Merchant Shipping and Foreign Enlistment was discussed, but it was generally thought by the majority of the court not to be clear enough to establish criminal jurisdiction over foreign nationals within three miles of the coasts without specifically addressing that point.

In one of the commentaries, which seems ironic in the light of later history, it was noted that in the negotiations preceded the Treaty of Intervention in 1840, Russia had objected to the closure by Turkey of the Straits of the Dardanelles –

> "It was replied on the part of the British Government, that in its opinion respecting the navigation of these straits by the ships of war of foreign nations rested upon a general and fundamental principle of international law." Every state is considered as having territorial jurisdiction "over the sea which washes its shores as far as three miles from low-water mark; and consequently any strait, which is bounded on both sides by the territory of the same sovereign and which is not more than six miles wide, lies within the territorial jurisdiction of that sovereign."

Presumably by the time of Gallipoli and the Dardanelles attacks of the First World War, the British Government had changed its mind, or its priorities.

The dissenting judgement of Lord Coleridge, Chief Justice of Common Pleas, in *Keyn* also touched on a truly remarkable legal tussle that took place between Queen Victoria and Albert Edward Prince of Wales, later King Edward VII. This concerned the rights to the proceeds of mineral workings from mines in Cornwall – belonging to the Prince as

89

part of his landholdings in the Duchy of Cornwall. Some of the mines extended out beyond the foreshore under the seabed, and these were eventually found to belong to the Queen in right of her Crown.

The British unwritten constitution can be called many things, but modern is not one of them. Holding land in right of the Crown is an idea that dates back to feudal tenure, when the concept was that all land belonged to the King, and he allowed other nobles tenure of parts of it at will, usually in return for useful services such as raising armies for beating up the Scots or Welsh. The spectacle of a Royal mother and son referring their competing hereditary rights for resolution by sheaves of distinguished judges, and eventually by an Act of Parliament, must have been remarkable. The consequences of the issue, however, are of enormous commercial importance today. The Duchy of Cornwall is still a huge landowner in that County, and elsewhere in the United Kingdom, while the Crown Estate issues licences for activities on the Continental Shelf extending many miles out to sea, including offshore drilling for oil and gas and offshore wind farms.

Grove's dissenting judgement in *Keyn* pointed out the absurd result that in some circumstances the crime of murder might be prosecuted if it involved a foreign national in disputed waters, but not manslaughter. It was a point taken up by at least one of his fellow dissenters, and was well made. In the event, the majority of the court went the other way, but as international law and Treaties developed, the dissenters' judgement was fully justified.

These and so many other issues remained to be worked out from first principles. Today the point at issue in *Keyn* has been resolved by the United Nations Convention on the Law of the Sea, which establishes in international law states' rights to 12 miles of territorial waters, and their ability to declare 'Exclusive Economic Zones' extending up to 200 miles from their shores.

St Helens Chemical Company v The Corporation of St Helens, 1876, Grove J.

While in no way as important as the *Keyn* case, Grove's judgement in the case of *St Helens Chemical Company* in 1876 was an example of a

Victorian case of 'statutory nuisance' and the way in which it began to be used to deal with environmental problems.

The St Helens Chemical Company used two drains from its chemical works, one containing liquid impregnated with muriatic acid and the other liquid impregnated with sulphur. It saw nothing wrong with having these discharge to the sewer system maintained by the Corporation of St Helens. But the discharges combined to let off sulphuretted hydrogen, and eventually proceedings were taken against the chemical company for causing a statutory nuisance, as the gas escaped into adjoining houses. The company was convicted by magistrates and given 21 days to 'abate the nuisance', but appealed. It was the company's managers' bad luck to have their appeal heard by a judge who had been a member of the Metropolitan Commission on Sewers, and who probably knew more about sulphuretted hydrogen than they did.

Mr Justice Grove held that –

> "In my opinion the decision of the justices was right, and must be affirmed….It would be a singular result of the legislation as to the removal of nuisances, if the appellants could send from their works matter which, upon reaching a public sewer, is dangerous to the health of the inhabitants of the borough… The escape of a noxious gas like sulphuretted hydrogen is clearly a nuisance in ordinary language."

His fellow judge concurred, and the St Helens Chemical Company was obliged to embark upon cleaning up its factory discharges.

R v Gallagher and others – a Fenian Brotherhood Treason Felony trial, 1883

There are areas of history where it is hard to escape the feeling that there is nothing new under the sun, and that no one has learned anything at all from past events. Nothing does more to prompt this feeling than consideration of the history of terrorism, or as we say these days, the 'War on Terror'.

As Steven Runciman's *History of the Crusades* points out, the original Assassins were an obscure sect of Shia persuasion based in part in the Nosairi mountains and led from his castle at al-Kahf by Sheikh Sinan, known as the "Old Man of the Mountains". It would be interesting to know to what extent this horrible old man may have been a role model for Osama Bin Laden. Their fondness for advancing their foreign policy by means of selected assassination of kings, princes and passing crusaders was alternated by local alliances, even with the same crusaders. In 1194, Henry of Champagne was entertained to lunch and a demonstration of lower ranking assassins killing themselves on the orders of their sheikh, which has a very contemporary sound to it. Sometimes, however, the Assassins misjudged the prevailing mood and current political situation. Their decision to murder Genghis Khan's second son Jagatai in 1257 may be considered to have been a mistake, as it led to a Mongol horde under the general Hulagu being sent to wipe out the sect in Persia, which they did with great gusto and practiced efficiency.

The case of *The Queen v Thomas Gallagher and others* at the Central Criminal Court in London in 1883 prompts similar feelings of having 'been here before'. It considered whether individual acts of terrorism prepared and committed by Americans against Britain amounted to acts of war within the meaning of Treason-Felony Act of 1848.

Mr Justice Grove was chosen to join Lord Chief Justice Coleridge and the Master of the Rolls, the two most senior judges in England, to preside over this trial, and it is hard to see how this could possibly have happened if he did not enjoy considerable respect for having a cool head and sound legal judgement. There is no way of knowing whether the scientific aspects of the evidence led his fellow judges to select a scientist from amongst their number to help consider the evidence.

In the early 1880s, secret clubs were formed in America known as the "Fenian Brotherhood", whose express aim was to procure "the freedom of Ireland by force alone". Six Irish Americans were charged with having joined these clubs, and having travelled to England with funds, time and the means to destroy public buildings by the use of large amounts of nitro-glycerine and other explosives, which they were in the process of manufacturing in London and Birmingham when arrested. It appears that they had taken an unhealthy interest in the layout of the House of Commons, Scotland Yard and other potential targets.

The Treason-Felony Act of 1848 had established a new criminal offence, only one step down from the capital offence of high treason –

> *"If any person shall, within the United Kingdom or without, compass, imagine, invent, devise, or intend to deprive or depose our most gracious Lady the Queen, her heirs or successors, from the style, honour or royal name of the Imperial Crown of the United Kingdom or any other of Her Majesty's dominions or countries, or to levy war against Her Majesty, her heirs or successors, within any part of the United Kingdom, in order by force or constraint to compel her or them to change her or their measures or counsels, or in order to put any force or constraint upon, or in order to intimidate or overawe both Houses or either House of Parliament, or to move or stir any foreigner or stranger with force to invade the United Kingdom or any other of Her Majesty's dominions or countries under the obeisance of Her Majesty, her heirs or successors, and such compassings, imaginations, inventions, devices, or intentions, or any of them shall express, utter or declare by publishing any printing, or writing, or by open and advised speaking, or by any overt word or deed..."*

The penalty on conviction of such offences was to be transportation for life or not less than seven years, up to life imprisonment or prison for up to two years with or without hard labour.

The Attorney General of the day opened the case, explaining that Treason-Felony was very close to high treason, a statutory offence dating from 1848. The prisoners were charged with levying war against the Queen – not in the sense of raising "an array of men in military formation, attempting with weapons of war to attack the Queen's forces or fortresses". Instead, he argued –

> "It was sufficient for the levying of war if, by a force destructive of life or property – a force discovered by modern science – it was attempted to take the lives of the Queen's

subjects generally, and not with a personal or private object; if it were intended to destroy property for an unlawful and not a lawful purpose, that in itself would be a sufficient levying of war…"

One of the prisoners, William Joseph Lynch, also known as Norman, gave evidence that he was a coach painter by trade, living in Brooklyn, New York. He had been approached by one Daniel O'Connor to join the Emerald Club Branch of the Fenian Brotherhood, and had been taken to a meeting at the Oddfellows' Hall at Second Street, the Bowery, New York. In the presence of about thirty men he had taken an oath – "Stand by the watchword, obey the superior officers, and …preserve the funds of the Brotherhood", and kissed a book. After the administration of this rather poorly drafted oath, he was asked to pay two dollars, and thereafter 10 cents per week. He began to attend secret meetings weekly, meeting other Brotherhood members referred to only by numbers, or by names, including "the Old Man" - not in this case Sheikh Sinan of the Assassins, but one O'Donovan Rossa, with perhaps a similar outlook on life.

After this, the conspirators took ship to England, one of them, Thomas Gallagher, taking time out from his medical practice in Brooklyn, telling one witness that he was coming to England for the purpose of "walking the hospitals." One of them, Whitehead, set about making large purchases, amounting to 1,703lb of nitric acid, 3,306lb of sulphuric acid and 4cwt 50lbs of glycerine from a series of puzzled wholesale chemists and other suppliers. They purchased rubber bags and even a pair of fishing waders into which to pour the mixture.

Production of the nitro-glycerine was on such a scale that Whitehead even took a small shop in Birmingham, and advertised for a boy to help maintain the pretence of genuine trade – a mistake, as the 13 year old shop boy James Crowder later proved to be a telling witness –

"No one else was employed there but myself. There were paper, paint-brushes and paint in the shop. I never sold things myself, and I never saw much sold there. Whitehead worked in the back premises, and told me he was mixing paint…I observed that his nails and fingers were yellow."

94

An observant Police Sergeant, Richard Price, received information about the suspicious chemicals deliveries at the shop, and disguised as a painter made a test purchase there, noting that Whitehead's clothes were burnt with acid. He later let himself in with a skeleton key, and was sufficiently suspicious about what he found there that he went back with the Chief Constable and arrests were made.

The prisoners had made about 200lb of nitro-glycerine, of which Colonel Vivien Majendie, Her Majesty's Chief Inspector of Explosives would later say –

> "I think almost any known building would be destroyed with a less quantity than 200 lb."

Edward Clark Q.C. for Thomas Gallagher submitted that there was no evidence that the prisoners had been "levying war" against the Queen, which would have entailed being "arrayed and circumstanced in apposition to the public authority." So what were the prisoners doing? The presiding judges asked searching questions about what might amount to "levying war". Would a mine laid at Windsor Castle be enough?

> *"Grove J.* – Supposing the Channel tunnel be made and the French Government sent a set of men in ordinary dress, and they put down dynamite at different parts of the tunnel for the purpose of destroying the approach, and with a view to ultimately conquering this country, would that not be a levying of war on the part of France?
>
> *Clarke.* – It might be in the course of levying a war.
>
> *The Master of the Rolls.* – Would that be war or not?
>
> *Clarke.* – No, he would certainly say not. It was a conspiracy, a co-operation if they liked, for the purpose of destroying property.

Grove J. – With the intention of ultimately of conquering England."

The result of these debates was that the Lord Chief Justice gave the ruling that if the jury found that the prisoners or any of them had agreed among themselves that some of them should destroy the property of the Crown, and destroy or endanger the lives of Her Majesty's subjects by explosive materials, then the prisoners would be guilty of treason felony within the meaning of the Act. If three men with these explosive materials did the same acts with the same objects as it required 3,000 men to do in an earlier period, the acts of the three men to-day were equally a levying of war. Thomas Gallagher, Whitehead, Wilson and Curtin were found guilty and sentenced to penal servitude for life. Two other defendants, Ansburgh and Bernard Gallagher, were found not guilty.

Exactly similar issues arise today. Individuals or small groups of dedicated terrorists have the means to fly airliners into buildings or threaten capital cities with sarin poisoning, radioactive dirty bombs, semtex, suicide and car bombs. Does that mean that society, in its determination to respond to these acts of terror, is at "war", and to what extent do the acts of terrorism justify either a military response or wholesale suspension and infringement of individual liberties by legislation and the security apparatus of the state? The judgement of Grove and his fellow judges was a particular response concerning the application of specific legislation, but the arguments are not over yet.

The satirical journal *Vanity Fair* marked Grove's retirement in 1876 with a somewhat mocking account of his career as a scientist, lawyer and judge. It said that as an advocate –

> "Mr Grove...soon proved to the satisfaction of the litigating public that no patent or other case which might involve any scientific or chemical process was complete without him..."

The *Vanity Fair* article added tartly that Grove had been appointed to the Bench in 1871, and that it was not his fault that this appointment had been fifteen years later than it should have been. The article stated that Mr Justice Grove –

"...thenceforth proceeded to dispense a mixture of equal parts of science and law to an ordinary public with considerable discrimination and some success...until last month, when he retired from public life full of honours and years. He might have been a better judge had he been made one earlier in life...."

The magazine recorded that –

"He has always been noted for his industry and for an amount of imperturbable good humour which has made him a general favourite with the Bar, and kept him so, even when his faculties had become slow and his science old-fashioned."

Grove was, they declared –

"A very nice old gentleman of the olden school...he has plenty of friends and deserves them all. It is doubtful whether his name will live longest in law or in science, but it is a fact that his science never enabled him to master the intricacies of the Judicature Acts. By his retirement he has shown himself to be possessed of much sound sense."

This was accompanied by a caricature of Grove under the heading "galvanic electricity", in the robes, wig and whiskers of high Victorian judicial style, and without knowing more about him, it is hard to make out the lively character of the scientist depicted in the earlier photographs, or the forceful advocate. This rather catty summary of Grove's achievements in sixteen years on the High Court Bench may not do him full justice, and certainly underestimates the continuing need for "sound sense" in the upper reaches of the judiciary. The examples given above of Grove's work as a judge may serve to show that sense applied to some of the most important legal issues of his day.

Grove died in 1896, and his funeral took place very quietly at Kensal Green cemetery. The *Law Times* noted that his personal estate of £215,900 was the largest of any member of the legal profession reported that year. It seems that for all his disdain or disinterest in the commercial applications of science, Grove had achieved his object of securing his family's future by pursuing a successful legal career.

History has been even less kind to *Vanity Fair's* dismissal of Grove's science as 'old fashioned'. The future of fuel cells and the Grove Fuel Cell Seminar held every two years in London have shown him to be about 160 years ahead of his time.

APPENDIX 1

ANTAGONISM

Grove's last, and most famous, Friday Evening Discourse at the Royal Institution, delivered when he was 78.

WEEKLY EVENING MEETING,
Friday, April 20, 1888
Edward Woods, Esq. M. Inst. C.E. Vice President, in the Chair.

The Right. Hon. SIR WILLIAM R. GROVE, M.A. D.C.L. LL.D.
F.R.S. M.R.I

Antagonism

Some months ago, shortly after I had resigned my office of Judge of the High Court, I was expressing to a friend my fear of the effect of having no compulsory occupation, when he said, by way of consolation, "Never mind, 'for Satan finds some mischief still for idle hands to do.' " You may possibly in the course of the evening think he was right.

I have chosen a title for my lecture which may not fully convey to your minds the scope of the views which I am going to submit to you. I propose to adduce some arguments to show that "antagonism," a word generally used to signify something disagreeable, pervades all things; that it is not the baneful thing which many consider it; that it produces at least quite as much good as evil; but that, whatever be its effect, my theory - call it, if you will, speculation - is that it is a necessity of existence, and of the organism of the universe so far as we understand it; that motion in life cannot go on without it; that it is not a mere casual adjunct of Nature, but that without it there would be no Nature, at all events as we conceive it; that it is inevitably associated with unorganised matter, with organised matter, and with sentient beings.

I am not aware that this view, in the breadth in which it I suggest it, has been advanced before. Probably no idea is new in all respects in the present period of the world's history. It has been said by a desponding pessimist that "There is nothing new, and nothing true, and nothing signifies," but I do not entirely agree with him; I believe that in what I am about to submit there is something new and true in the point of view from which I regard the matter; whether it signifies or not is for you to judge.

The universality of antagonism has not received the attention it seems to me to deserve from the fact of the element of force, or rather of the conquering force, being mainly attended to and too little note taken of the element of resistance unless the latter vanquishes the force, and then it becomes, popularly speaking, the force, and the former force the resistance.

There are propositions applying more or less to what I am going to say of some antiquity.

Heraclitus, quoted by Prof. Huxley, said: "War is the father and king of all things." Hobbes said war is the natural state of man, but his expressions have about them some little ambiguity. In Chapter 1. of the 'De Corpore Politico' he says, "Irresistible might in a state of nature is right," and "The estate of man in this natural liberty is war." Subsequently he says: "A man gives up his natural right, for when divers men having right not only to all things else, but to one another's persons, if they use the same there ariseth thereby invasion on the one part and resistance on the other, which is war, and therefore *contrary to the law of Nature, the sum whereof consisteth in making peace."* I can only explain this apparent inconsistency by supposing he meant "law of Nature" to be something different from "the natural estate of man," and that the making peace was the fist effort at contract, or the beginning of law; but then why call it the *"law of Nature,"* where he says might is right? There is some obscurity in the passage.

The Persian divinities, Ormuzd and Ahriman, were the supposed rulers or representatives of good and evil, always at war, and causing the continuous struggles between human beings animated respectively by these two principles. Undoubtedly good and evil are antagonistic, but antagonism, as I view it, is as necessary to good as to evil, as necessary to Ormuzd as to Ahriman. Zoroaster's religion of a Divine being, one and indivisible, but with two sides, is, to my mind, a more philosophical conception. The views of Lamarck on the modification of

100

organic beings by effort, and the establishment of the doctrine of Darwin as to the effects produced by the struggle for existence and domination, come much nearer to my subject. Darwin has shown how these struggles have modified the forms and habits of organised beings, and tended to increase differentiation, and Prof. Huxley and Herbert Spencer have powerfully promoted and expanded these doctrines. To the latter we owe the happy phrase, "survival of the fittest," and Prof. Huxley has recently, in a paper in the 'Nineteenth Century,' anticipated some points I should have adverted to as to the social struggles for existence. To be anticipated, and by a very short period, is always trying, but it is more trying when what you intended to say has been said by your predecessor in more terse and appropriate language than you have at your command.

I propose to deal with "antagonism" inductively, i.e. with facts derived from observation alone, and not to meddle with spiritual matters or with consequences.

Let us begin with what we know of the visible universe, viz. suns, planets, comets, meteorites, and their effects. These are all pulling at each other, and resisting that pull by the action of other forces.

Any change in this pulling force produces a change, or, as it is called, perturbation, in the motion of the body pulled. The planet Neptune, as you know, was discovered by the effect of its pulling force on another planet, the latter being deflected from its normal course. When this pulling force is not counterbalanced by other forces, or when the objects pulled have not sufficient resisting power, they fall into each other. Thus, this earth is daily causing a bombardment of itself by drawing smaller bodies - meteorites - to it, 20,000,000 of which, visible to the naked eye, fall on average into our atmosphere in each twenty-four hours, and of those visible through the telescope, 400,000,000 are computed to fall within the same period. Mr. Lockyer has recently given reasons for supposing the luminosity of nebulae, or of many of them, is due to collisions or friction among the meteorites which go to form them; but his paper on the subject is not yet published. You must get from Mr. Lockyer the details of his views. I hope he may, at one of these evening meetings, give you a *resume* of them from the place I now occupy.

What is commonly called centrifugal force does not come from nothing; it depends upon the law that a body falling by the influence of attraction, not upon, but near to, the attracting body, whirls round the latter, describing one of the curves known as conic sections. Hence a meteorite may become a planet or satellite (one was supposed to have become so to this earth, but I believe the observations have not been verified); or it may go off in a parabola as comets do; or again, this centrifugal force may be generated by the gradual accretion of nebulous matter into solid masses falling near to, or being thrown off from the central nucleus, the two forces (centrifugal and centripetal) being antagonistic to each other, and the relative movements being continuous, but probably not perpetual. Our solar system is also kept in its place by the antagonism of the surrounding bodies of the Kosmos pulling at us. Suppose half of the stars we see, i.e. all on one side of a meridian line, were removed, what would become of our solar system? It would drift away to the side where attraction still existed, and there would be a wreck of matter and a crash of worlds. It is very little known that Shakespeare was acquainted with this pulling force. He says, by mouth of Cressida -

"But the strong base and building of my love
Is as the very centre of the earth,
Drawing all things to it" -

A very accurate description of the law of gravitation, so far as this earth is concerned, and written nearly a century before Newton's time.

But in all probability the collisions of meteorites with the earth and other suns and planets are not the only collisions in space. I know of no better theory to account for the phenomena of temporary stars, such as that which appeared in 1866, than that they result from the collision of non-luminous stars, or stars previously invisible to us. That star burst suddenly into light, and then the luminosity gradually faded, the star became more and more dim and ultimately disappeared. The spectrum of it showed that the light was compound, and had probably emanated from two different sources. It was probably of a very high temperature. If this theory of temporary stars be admitted, we get a nebula of vapour

102

or star dust again, and so may get fresh instances of the nebular hypothesis.

Let us now take the earth itself. It varies in temperature, and consequently the particles at or near its surface are in continuous movement, rubbing against each other, being oxidised or deoxidised, either immediately or through the medium of vegetation. This also is continuously tearing up its surface and changing its character. Evaporation and condensation, producing rain, hail, and storms, notably change it. Force and resistance are constantly at play. The sea erodes rocks and rubs them into sand. The sea quits them, and leaves traces of its former presence by the fossil marine shells found now at high altitudes. Rocks crumble down and break other rocks or are broken by them; avalanches are not uncommon. The interior of the earth seems to be in a perpetual state of commotion, though only recurrent to our observation. Earthquakes in various places from time to time, and doubtless many beneath the sea of which we are not cognizant, nor of other gradual upheavals and depressions. Throughout it nothing that we know of is at rest, and nothing can move without changing the position of something else, and this is antagonism. Metals rust at its surface, and probably they or their oxides, chlorides, &c., are in a continuous state of change in the interior. Nothing that we know of is stationary. The earth as a whole seems so at first sight, but its surface is moving at the rate of some seventeen miles a minute at the equator; and standing at either of the poles - an experiment which no one has yet had an opportunity of trying - a man would be turned round his own axis once in every twenty four hours, while the earth's motion round the sun carries us through space more than a million and a half miles a day.

The above changes produce motion in other things. The earth pulls the sun and planets, and in different degrees at different portions of its orbit.

Before I pass from inorganic to organized matter I had better deal with what may perhaps strike you as the most difficult part of my subject, viz. light. Where, you may say, is there antagonism in the case of light? Light exercises its force upon such minute portions of matter that until the period of the discovery of photography its physical and chemical effects were almost unknown. Such effects as bleaching, uniting some gases, and affecting the colouring matter of vegetables, were partially known but little attended to; but photography created a new era: I shall advert to this presently. The theories of light, however, involved matter and motion. The corpuscular theory, as you well know, supposed that excessively small particles were emitted from luminous bodies, and travelled with enormous velocity. The undulatory theory, which supplanted it, supposed that luminous bodies caused undulations or vibrations in a highly tenuous matter called ether, which is supposed to exist throughout the interplanetary spaces and throughout the universe so far as we know it. Some suppose this ether to be of a specific character differing from that of ordinary gases, others that it is in the nature of a highly attenuated gas; but, whatever it be, it cannot be affected by undulations or vibrations without being moved, and when matter is moved by any force it must offer resistance to that force, and hence we get antagonism between force and resistance. Light also takes time in overcoming this resistance, i.e. in pushing aside the ether. It travels, no doubt, at a good pace - about 190,000 miles in a second; but even at this rate, and without being particular as to a few millions of miles, it takes three years and a quarter to reach us from the star which, so far as we know, is the nearest to us, viz. a Centauri. The ether, or whatever it may be called, tenuous as it is, is not unimportant, though it be not heavy. Without it we should have no light and possibly no heat, and the consequences of its absence would be rather formidable. I believe you have heard Dr. Tyndall on this subject. Supposing the visible universe to be as it is now supposed to be, i.e. in no part a mere vacuum, there can be no force without resistance in any part of it.

But photography carries us further, it shows us that light acts on matter chemically, that it is capable of decomposing or forcing asunder the constituents of chemical compounds, and is therefore a force met by resistance. In the year 1856 I made some experiments, published in the 'Philosophical Magazine' for January 1857, which seemed to me to carry still further what I may call the molecular fight between light and chemical affinity, and among them the following. Letters cut out of paper are placed between two polished squares of glass with tin-foil on the outsides. It is then electrized like a Leyden jar, for a few seconds, the glasses separated, the letters blown off, and the inside of one of the glasses covered with photographic collodion. This is then exposed to diffuse daylight, and on being immersed in the nitrate of silver bath the part which had been covered with the paper comes out dark, the remainder of the plate being unaffected. (This result was shown by the electric light lantern.) In this case we see that another imponderable force, electricity, invisibly affects the surface of glass in such a way that it conveys to another substance of definite thickness, viz. the prepared collodion, a change in the chemical relations of the substance (iodide of silver) pervading it, enabling it to resist that decomposition by light which but for some unseen modification of the surface of the glass plate it would have undergone, and no doubt the force of light being unable to effect its object was reflected or dispersed, and instead of changing its mode of motion in effecting chemical decomposition, it goes off on other business. The visible effect is in the collodion film alone. I have stripped that off, and the imprint remains on it, the surface of the glass being, so far as I could ascertain, unaffected. Thus in the film over the protected part, light conquers chemical affinity; in that over the non-protected part, chemical affinity resists and conquers light, which has to make an ignominious retreat. It is a curious chapter in the history of the struggles of molecular forces, and probably similar contests between light and chemical or physical attractions go on in many natural phenomena, some forms of blight and some healthy vegetable changes being probably dependent on the varying effects of light, and conditions, electrical or otherwise, of the atmosphere.

Let us now pass on to organic life. A blade of grass, as Burke, I believe, said as a figure of speech, is fighting with its neighbours. It is robbing them, and they are trying to rob it - no agreement or contract, simply force opposed to force. This struggle is good for the grass; if it got too much nutriment it would become diseased. The struggle keeps it in health. The rising of sap in trees, the assimilation of carbon, the process of growth, the strengthening themselves to resist prevalent winds, and many other instances might be given, which afford examples of the internal and external struggles in vegetable life.

I will now proceed to consider animal life, and in this case I will begin with the internal life of animals, which is a continual struggle. That great pump the heart is continuously beating - that is, conquering resistance. It is forcing the blood through the arteries, they assist in squeezing it onwards. If they give way, the animal dies; if they become rigid and resist too much, the animal dies. There must be a regulated antagonism, a rhythmical pulsation, the very term involving force and resistance. That the act of breathing is antagonistic scarcely needs argument. The muscular action by which the ribs are made to open out and close alternately, in order to inhale and exhale air, and other physiological changes which I cannot here go into, necessitate a continuous fight for life. So with digestion, assimilation, and other functions, mechanical and chemical forces and resistances come into play.

Since this lecture was written, I have heard of a discovery made, I am informed, by Prof. Metschnikoff, and which was brought to light a singular instance of internal antagonism. He is said to have proved that the white corpuscles of the blood are permanent enemies of Bacteria, and by inoculation will absorb poisonous germs; a recurrent war, as it appears, going on between them. If the corpuscle is the conqueror, the Bacteria are swallowed up, and the patient lives. If the corpuscles are vanquished, the patient dies, and the Bacteria live, at all events for a time. If the theory is founded, it affords a strong additional argument to the doctrine of internal antagonism. Possibly if there were no Bacteria, and the corpuscles had nothing to do, it would be worse for them and the animal whom they serve.

Let us now consider the external life of animals. I will take as an instance, for a reason which you will soon see, the life of a wild rabbit. It is throughout its life, except when asleep (of which more presently), using exertion, cropping grass, at war with vegetables, &c. If it gets a luxurious pasture it dies of repletion. If it gets too little it dies of inanition. To keep itself healthy it must exert itself for its food; this, and perhaps the avoiding its enemies, gives its exercise and care, brings all its organs into use, and thus it acquires its most perfect form of life. I have witnessed this effect myself, and that is the reason why I choose the rabbit as an example. An estate in Somersetshire, which I once took temporarily, was on the slope of the Mendip Hills. The rabbits on the one part of it, viz. that on the hillside, were in perfect condition, not too fat nor too thin, sleek, active, and vigorous, and yielding to their antagonists, myself and family, excellent food. Those in the valley, where the most pasturage was rich and luxuriant, were all diseased, most of them unfit for human food, and many lying dead on the fields. They had not to struggle for life, their short life was miserable and their death early, they wanted the sweet uses of adversity - that is, of antagonism.

The same story may be told of other animals. Carnivora, beasts or birds of prey, live on weaker animals; weaker animals herd together to resist, or, by better chance of warning, to escape, beasts of prey; while they, the Herbivora, in their turn are destroying vegetable organisms.

I now come to the most delicate part of my subject, viz. man (I include women of course!) Is man exempt from this continual struggle?

It is needless to say that war is antagonism. Is not peace so also, though in a different form? It is common-place remark to say that the idle man is worn out by *ennui*, i.e. by internal antagonism. Kingsley's "Do-as-you-like" race-who were fed by a substance dropping from trees, who did no work, and who gradually degenerated until they became inferior to apes, and ultimately died out from having nothing to do, nothing to struggle with-is a caricature illustrative of the matter. That the worry of competition is nearly equivalent to the hardships and perils of military life, seems proved to me by the readiness with which military life is voluntarily undertaken, ill as it is paid. If it were well paid, half our men would be in the military or naval service, and I am not sure that we should not have regiments of Amazons! The increased risk of life or limbs and the arduous nature of the work do not prevent men belonging to all classes from entering these services, little remunerative as they are. Others take the risks of travelling in the deserts of Africa or wintering in the polar regions, of being eaten by lions or frozen to death, of falling from a Swiss mountain or foundering in a yacht, in preference to a life of tranquillity; and sportsmen prefer the danger of endeavouring to kill an animal that can and may kill them, to shooting tame pheasants at a *battue* or partridges in a turnip-field.

Then, in what is euphemistically called a life of peace, buyer and seller, master and servant, landlord and tenant, debtor and creditor, are all in a state of simmering antagonism; and the inventions and so-called improvements of applied science and art do not lessen it. Exercise is antagonism; at each step force is used to lift up our bodies and push back the earth; as the eminent Joseph Montgolfier said, that when he saw a company dancing, he mentally inverted his view and imagined the earth dancing on the dancers' feet, which it most unquestionably did. Indeed, his great invention of balloons was guessed at by his witnessing a mild form of antagonism between heat and gravitation. He, being a dutiful husband, was airing his wife's dresses, who was going to a ball. He observed the hot air from the fire inflated the light materials, which rose up in a sort of spheroidal form (you may some of you have noticed this form in dress!). This gave him the idea of the fire-balloon, which being a large paper-maker at Annonay, he forthwith experimented on, and hence we got aërial navigation. This anecdote was told me by his nephew M. Seguin, also an eminent man. Even what we call a natural death is a greater struggle than that which other animals go through, and is, in fact, the most artificial of all deaths. The lower animals, practically speaking, do experience a natural death, i.e. a violent or unforeseen death. As soon as their powers decline to such an extent that they cannot take part in the struggle for existence, they die or are killed, generally quickly, and their sufferings are not protracted by the artificial tortures arising from the endeavours to prolong life.

Let us now pass from individuals to communities. Is there less antagonism now than of yore? Do the nations of Europe now form a happy family? Are the armaments of Continental nations, or is the navy of this country, less than in former years? The very expression "the Great Powers" involves antagonism.

As with wars and revolutions, so, as I have said, with regard to individuals, during our so-called peace, the fight is continuous among communities. If the water does not boil, it simmers. Not merely are there the struggles of poor against rich going on, but the battles for position and pre-eminence are constant. The subjugated party or sect seeks first for toleration, then for equalisation, and then for domination.

We call contentment a virtue, but we inculcate discontent. A father reproaches his son for not exerting himself to improve his position, and at school and college and in subsequent periods of life efforts at advancement in the social scale are recommended. Individual antagonisms, class antagonisms, political, trading, and religious antagonisms take the place of war. Can war exhibit a more vigorous and persistent antagonism than competition does? Take the college student with ruined health; take the bankrupt tradesman with ruined family; take the aspirants of fashion turning night into day, and preferring gas or electric light to that of the sun: there is, to be sure, some excuse for this, as we so rarely see the latter.

But our very amusements are of a combative character: chess, whist, billiards, racing, cricket, football, &c. And in all these we, in common parlance, speak of *beating* our opponent. Even dancing is probably a relic and reminiscence of war, and some of its forms are of a military character. I can call to mind only one game which is not combative, and that is the game you are in some sort now playing, viz. "patience" and with, I fear, some degree of internal antagonism!

Take, again, the ordinary incidents of a day's life in London: 15,000 to 20,000 cabs, omnibuses, vans, private carriages, &c., all struggling, the horses pushing the earth back and themselves forwards, the pedestrians doing the same, but the horses compulsorily – they have not yet got votes. The occupants of the cabs, vans &c., are supposed to act from free will, but in the majority of cases they are as much driven as the horses. Insolvents trying to renew bills, rich men trying to save what they have got by saving half an hour of time. Imagine, if you can, the friction of all this, and add the bargaining in shops, the mental efforts in counting-houses, banks, &c., and road repair, now a permanent and continuous institution. Take our railways: similar efforts and resistances. Drivers, signal-men, porters, &c., and the force emanating from the sun millions of years ago, and locked up in the coal-fields, as Stephenson suggested, now employed to overcome the inertia of trains and to make them push the earth in this or that direction, and themselves along its surface. Take the daily struggles in commerce, law, professions, and legislation, and sometimes even in science and literature. Politics I cannot enter upon here, but must leave you to judge whether there is not some degree of antagonism in its pursuit. In all this there is plenty of useful antagonism, plenty of useless - much to please Ormuzd and much to delight Ahriman; but of the two extremes, over-work or stagnation, the latter would, I think, do Ahriman's work more efficiently than the former. We cry peace when there is no peace. Would the world, however, be better if it were otherwise? Is the Nirvana a pleasing prospect? Sleep, though not without its troubles and internal antagonism, is our nearest approach to it, but we should hardly wish to be always asleep.

Shakespeare not only knew something about gravitation, but he also knew something about antagonism. He says, by the mouth of Agamemnon -

> "Sith every action that hath gone before,
> Whereof we have record, trial did draw,
> Bias and thwart, not answering the aim,
> And that unbodied figure of the thought
> That gave't surmised shape."

In no case is the friction of life shown more than in the performance of "duty," i.e. an act of self-resistance, a word very commonly used; but the realisation of it is by no means so frequent. Indeed, faith in its performance so yields to scepticism that it is said that when a man talks of doing his duty, he is meditating some knavish trick.

The words good and evil are correlative: they are like height and depth, parent and offspring. You cannot, as far as I can see, conceive the existence of one without involving the conception of the other. In their common acceptation they represent the antagonism between what is agreeable or beneficial and what is painful or injurious.

An old anecdote will give us the notion of good and evil in a slenderly educated mind. A missionary having considered that he had successfully inculcated good principles in the mind of a previously untutored savage, produced him for exhibition before a select audience, and began his catechism by asking him the nature of good and evil. "Evil," the pupil answered, "is when other man takes my wife." "Right," said the missionary, "now give me an example of good." The answer was: "Good is when me takes other man's wife." The answer was not exactly what was expected, but was not far in disaccord with modern views among ourselves and other so-called civilised races. I don't mean as to running away with other men's wives! But we still view good and evil very much as affecting our own interests. At the commencement of a war each of the opposing parties view victory - i.e. the destruction of their enemies - as good, and being vanquished as evil. Congregations pray for this. Statesmen invoke the God of battles. Those among you who are old enough will call to mind the Crimean war. Each combatant nation gives thanks for the destruction of the enemy, each side possibly believing that they respectively are in the right, but in reality not troubling themselves much about that minor question. We (unconsciously perhaps) "compound for sins we are inclined to, by damning those we have no mind to." So in the daily life of what is called peace. The stage-coach proprietor rejoiced when he had driven his rival off the road, railway directors and shareholders now do the same, so do publicans, shopkeepers, and other rivals. We are still permeated by the old notion of good and evil. But "antagonism," as I view it, not only comprehends the relation of good and evil, but, as I have said, produces both, and is as necessary to good as to evil. Without it there would be neither good nor evil.

Judging of the lives of our progenitors from what we see of the present races of men of less cerebral development, we may characterize them as having been more impulsive than ourselves, and as having their joys and sorrows more quickly alternated. After the hunt for food, accompanied by privation and suffering, comes the feast to gorging. Their main evil was starvation, their good repletion. Even now the Esquimaux watches a seal-hole in the bitter cold for hours and days, and his compensation is the spearing and eating the seal. The good is resultant upon and in the long run I suppose, equivalent to the evil. These men look not back into the past, and forward into the future as we do. We, by extending our thought over a wider area, are led to more continuing sacrifices, and aim at more lasting enjoyment in the result. The child suffers at school in order that his future life may be more prosperous. The man spends the best part of his life in arduous toil, physical or mental, in order that he may not want in his later years, or that his family may reap the benefit of his labour. Further-seeing men spend their whole lives on work little remunerative that succeeding generations may be benefited. The prudent man transmits health and wealth to his descendants, the improvident man poverty or gout. One main element of what we call civilisation is the capability of looking further back into the past, and further forward into the future; but, though measured on a different scale, the average antagonism and approximate equivalence appear to me to be the same.

Can we suppose a state of things either in the organic or the inorganic world, which, consistently with our experience or any deduction drawn from it, would be without antagonism? In the inorganic world it would be the absence of all movement, or, what practically amounts to the same thing, movement of everything in the same direction, and the same relative velocity; for, as movement is only known to us by relation, movement where nothing is stationary or moving in a different direction or with a different velocity would be unrecognizable.

So in the organic but non-sentient world, if there were no struggle, no absorption of food, no growth, nothing to overcome, there would be nothing to call life. If, again, in the sentient world there were no appetites, no hopes - for both these involve discontent - no fear, no good or bad, what would life be? If fully carried out, is not life without antagonism no life at all, a barren metaphysical conception of existence, or rather alleged conception, for we cannot present to the mind a form of such conception.

In the most ordinary actions, such as are necessary to sustain existence, we find, as I have already pointed out, a struggle more or less intense, but we also find a reciprocal interdependence of effort and result. The graminivorous animal is during his waking hours always at work, always making a small but continuous effort, selecting his pastures, cropping vegetables, avoiding enemies, &c. The Carnivora suffer more in their normal existence; their hunger is greater, and their physical exertion when they are driven by hunger to make efforts to obtain food is more violent than with the Herbivora, if they capture their prey by speed or battle, or their mental efforts are greater if they capture it by craft. But then their gratification is also more intense, and thus there is a sort of rough equation between their pain and their pleasure, the more sustained the labour the more permanent the gratification.

As, with food or exercise, deficiency is as injurious in one, as is excess in another direction, so as affecting the mind of communities, as I have stated it to be with individuals, the effect of a life of ease and too much repose is as much to be avoided as a life of unremitting toil. The Pitcairn islanders, who managed in some way to adapt their wants to their supply and to avoid undue increase of population, are said never to have reached old age. In consequence of the uneventful, unexcited lives they led, they died of inaction, not from deficiency of food or shelter, but of excitement. They should have migrated to England! They died as hares do when their ears are stuffed with cotton, i.e. from want of anxiety. We have hope in our suffering, and in the mid gush of our pleasure something bitter surges up.

"We look before and after, and pine for what is not,
Our sincerest laughter with some pain is fraught,
Our sweetest songs are those which tell of saddest thought."

The question may possibly occur to you, have we more or less antagonism now than in former times? We certainly have more complexity, more differentiation, in our mental characteristics, and probably in our physical, so far as the structure of the brain is concerned; but is there less antagonism? With greater complexity come increased wants, more continuous cares. Higher cerebral development is accompanied with greater nervous irritability, with greater social intricacies - we have more frequent petty annoyances, and they affect us more. With all our so-called social improvements, is there not the same struggle between crime and its repression? If we have no longer highway robberies, how many more cases of fraud exist, most of it not touched by our criminal laws? As to litigation I am perhaps not an impartial judge, but it seems to me that if law were as cheap as is desired, every next-door neighbour would be in litigation. It would seem as if social order had never more than the turn of the scale which is necessary to social existence in its favour when contrasted with the disorganizing forces. Without that there would be perpetual insurrections and anarchy. But though antagonism takes a different form it is still there. Are wars more regulated by justice that of yore? I venture to doubt it, though probably many may disagree with me. National self-interest or self-aggrandisement is, I think, the predominant factor, and is frequently admittedly so. I also doubt if the old maxim, "If you wish for peace prepare for war," is of much value. Large armaments and improvements in the means of destruction (whose inventors are more thought of than the discoverers of natural truths) are as frequently the cause of war as of its prevention. Are wars less sanguinary with 100-ton guns than with bows and arrows? I cannot enter into statistics on this subject, but a sensible writer who has, viz. Mr. Finlaison, came to the conclusion that wars cease now as anciently, not in the ratio or the improvements in killing implements, but from exhaustion of men or means. Wars undoubtedly occur at more distant intervals, or the human race would become extinct. Probably the largely increased competition supplies their place: we fight commercially more and militarily less. It is a sad reflection that man is almost the only animal that fights, not for food or means of life or for perpetuating its race, but from motives of the merest vanity, ambition or passion. War is, however, not wholly evil. It develops noble qualities - courage, endurance, self - sacrifice, friendship, &c. - and tends to get rid of the silly encumbrances of fashion and ostentation. But do the much be praised inventions of peace bring less antagonism? Consider the enormous labour and waste of time due to competition in the advertising system alone. Paper-making, type-founding, printing, pasting, posting or otherwise circulating, sandwich-men, &c., all at work for purposes which, I venture to think, are in great part useless; and those who might add to the productiveness of the earth, or to the enriching our knowledge, are helping to extend the limits of the black country, and wasting their time in interested self-laudation. And the consumer pays the costs. "Buy my clothing, which will never wear out." "Become a shareholder in our company, which will pay cent. per cent." "Take my pills, which will cure all diseases," &c. These eulogies come from these highly impartial persons the advertisers, all promising golden rewards, but, as with the alchemists, on condition, that gold be paid in advance for their wares; and the silly portion of the public (no small body) take them at their word. Though you may not fully agree with this my anathema of the advertising system, and though there may be some modicum of good in it, I think you will agree that it affords a notable illustration of antagonism. If I were a younger man, I think I should go to Kamchatka to avoid the penny post; possibly I should not be satisfied when I got there.

Civilisation begins by supplying wants, and ends by creating them, and each supply for the newly created want begets other wants, and so on, "*toties, quoties.*" As far as we can judge by its present progress, mankind seems tending to an automatic state. The requirements of each day are becoming so numerous as to occupy the greater portion of that day; and when telegrams, telephones, electro-motion, and numerous other innovations which will probably follow these, reach their full development, no time will be left for thought, repose or any

114

spontaneous individual action. In this mechanical state of existence in times of peace, extremes of joy and sorrow, of good and evil, will become more rare, and the necessary uniformity of life will reduce passion and feeling to a continuous petty friction. The converse of the existence contemplated by the Stoics will be attained, and instead of a life of calm contemplation, our successors will have a life of objectless activity. The end will be swallowed up in the means. It will be all pursuit and no attainment. Is there a *juste milieu*, a point at which the superfluous *commoda vitae* will cease? None probably would agree at where that point should be fixed, and the future alone can show whether the human race will emancipate itself from being, like Frankenstein, the slave of the monster it has created.

In the cases I have given as illustrations - and many more might be adduced - the evil resulting from apparently beneficial changes is not a mere accident: it is as necessary a consequence as reaction is a consequence of action. In the struggle for existence or supremacy inevitable in all social growths, the invention, enactment, &c., intended to remedy an assumed evil will be taken advantage of by those for whom it is not intended; the real grievance will have been exaggerated by those having an interest in trading on it, and the remedy itself will have collateral results not contemplated by those who introduce the change. I could give many instances of this by my own experience as an advocate and judge, but this would lead me away from my subject. Evils, indeed, result from the very change of habit induced by the alleged improvement. The carriage, which saves fatigue, induces listlessness, and tends to prevent healthy exercise. The knife and fork save the labour of mastication, but by their use there is not the same stimulus to the salivary glands, not the full healthy amount of secretion, whereby the digestion suffers; there is not the same exercise of the teeth whereby they are strengthened and uniformly worn, as we see in ancient skulls. It seems not improbable that their premature decay in civilised nations is due to the want of their normal exercise by the substitution of the knife and fork and stew - pan. According to the evolution theory, our organs have grown into what they are by long use, and the remission of this tends to irregular development, or atrophy. Every artificial appliance renders nugatory some pre-existing mode of action, either voluntary, or involuntary; and as the parts of the whole organism have become correlated, each part being modified by the functions and actions of the others, every part suffers more or less when the mode of action of any one part is changed. So with the social structure, the same correlation of its constituent parts is a necessary consequence of its growth, and the change of one part affects the well-being of other parts. All change, to be healthy, must be extremely slow, the defect struggling with the remedy through countless but infinitesimally minute gradations.

Lastly, do the forms of government give us any firm ground to rest upon as to there being less undue antagonism in one than in another form? Whether it is better to run a risk of, say, one chance in a thousand or more of being decapitated unjustly by a despot, or to have what one may eat or drink, or whom one may marry, decided by a majority of parish voters, is a question on which opinions may differ, but there is abundant antagonism in either case.

Communism, the dream of enthusiasts, offers little prospect of ease. It involves an unstable equilibrium, i.e. it consists of a chain of connection where a defect in one link can destroy the working of the whole system, and why the executive in that system should be more perfect than in others I have never been able to see. Antagonism, on the other hand, tends to stability. Each man working for his own interests helps to supply the wants of others, thus ministering to public convenience and order, and if one or more fail the general weal is not imperilled.

You may ask, Why this universal antagonism? My answer is, I don't know; Science deals only with the How? not with the Why? Why does matter gravitate to other matter, with a force inversely as the square of distance? Why does oxygen unite with hydrogen? All I can say is that antagonism is, to my mind, universal, and will, I believe, some day be considered as much a law as the law of gravitation. If matter is, as we believe, everywhere, even in the interplanetary space, and if it attracts and moves other matter, which it apparently must do, there must be friction or antagonism of some kind. So with organized beings, Nature only recognizes the right, or rather the power, of the strongest. If twenty men be wrecked on a secluded island which will only support ten, which ten have a right to the produce of the island? Nature gives no voice, and the strongest take it. You further ask me, *Cui bono?* what is

116

the use of this disquisition? I should answer, If the views be true, it is always useful to know the truth. The greatest discoveries have appeared useless at the time. Kepler's discovery of the relations of the planetary movements appeared of no use at the time: no one would now pronounce it useless. I can, however, see much probable utility in the doctrine I have advocated. The conviction of the necessity of antagonism, and that without it there would be no light, heat, electricity, or life, may teach us (assuming free will) to measure effort by the probable result and to estimate the degree of probability. It may teach us not to waste our powers on fruitless objects, but to utilise and regulate this necessity of existence; for, if my views are correct, too much or too little is bad, and a due proportion is good (like many other useful things, it is best in moderation), to accept it rather as a boon than a bane, and to know that we cannot do good without effort - that is, without some suffering.

I have spoken of antagonism pervading the universe. Is there, you may ask, any limit in point of time or space to force? If there be so, there must be a limit to antagonism. It is said that heat tends to dissipate itself, and all things necessarily to acquire a uniform temperature. This would in time tend practically, though not absolutely, to the annihilation of force and to universal death; but if there be evidence of this in our solar system and what we know of some parts of the universe, which is probably but little, is there is no conceivable means of reaction or regeneration of active heat? There is some evidence of a probable zero of temperature for gases as we know them, i.e. a temperature so low that at it matter could not exist in a gaseous form; but passing over gases and liquids, if matter becomes solid by loss of heat, such solid matter would coalesce, masses would be formed, these would gravitate to each other, and come into collision. It would be the nebular hypothesis over again. Condensations and collisions would again generate heat; and so on *ad infinitum*.

Collisions in the visible universe are probably more frequent than is usually supposed. New nebulae appear where there were none before, as recently in the constellation of Andromeda. Mr. Lockyer, as I have said, considers that they are constant in the nebulae; and if there be such a number of meteorites as are stated to fall daily into the atmosphere of this insignificant planet, what numbers must thereto be in the universe? There must be a sort of fog of meteorites, and this may account, coupled with possibly some dissipation of light or change of it into other forces, for the smaller degree of light than would be expected if the universe of stellar bodies were infinite. For if so, and stars are to be assumed to be of an equal average brightness, then if there be no loss or obstruction, as light from a star decreases as the square of the distance and would from an infinite number of stars probably increase in the same ratio, the night would be as brightly illuminated as the day. We are told that there are stars of different ages - nascent, adolescent, mature, decaying, and dying; and when some of them, like nations at war, are broken up by collision into fragments or resolved into vapour, the particles fight as individuals do, and like them end by coalescing and forming new suns and planets. As the comparatively few people who die in London to-night do not affect us here, so in the visible universe one sun or planet in a billion or more may die every century and not be missed, while another is being slowly born out of nebula. Thus worlds may be regenerated by antagonism without having for the time more effect upon the Kosmos than the people now dying in London have on us. I do not venture to say that these collisions are in themselves sufficient to renew solar life; time may give us more information. There may be other modes of regeneration or renewed activity of the dissipated force, and some of a molecular character. The conversion of heat into atomic force has been suggested by Mr. Crookes. I give no opinion on that, but I humbly venture to doubt the mortality of the universe.

Again as the universe is limited? and if so, by what? Not, I presume, by a stone wall! or if so, where does the wall end? Is space limited, and how? If space be unlimited and the universe of suns and planets, &c., limited, then the visible universe becomes a luminous speck in an infinity of dark vacuous space, and the gases, or at all events the so-called ether, unless limited in elasticity, would expand into this vacuum - a limited quantity of ether into an infinite vacuum! If the universe of matter be unlimited in space, then the cooling down may be unlimited in time. But these are perhaps fruitless speculations. We cannot comprehend infinity, neither can we conceive a limitation to it. I must once more quote Shakespeare, and say in his words, "It is past the infinite of thought." But whatever be the case with some stars and planets, I cannot bring myself to believe in a dead universe surrounded by a dark ocean of frozen ether.

Most of you have read 'Wonderland', and may recollect that after the Duchess has uttered some ponderous and enigmatical apophthegms, Alice says, "Oh!" "Ah," says the Duchess, "I could say a good deal more if I chose." So could I; but my relentless antagonist opposite (the clock) warns me, and I will only add one more word, which you will be glad to hear, and that word is - Finis.

[W. R. G.]

APPENDIX 2

Note on Grove's family, taken from Grove's Legal Obituary in the Law Times, 8th August 1896

…"He married in 1837 a daughter of Mr John Diston Powles who died in 1879. There were six children of the marriage – two sons and four daughters. The elder son is Mr F. Crauford Grove, a former President of the Alpine Club and the author of "The Frosty Caucasus" and of several plays, of which the best known is "Forget me Not"; and the younger, Coleridge Grove, after taking a first class in mathematics from Balliol went into the Army and is now a major-general and C.B. Of the daughters, one died unmarried; another married Mr Justice Hills, of the Supreme Court, Alexandria, and is the mother of Captain Hills, R.E. who has in no small measure inherited the scientific tastes of his grandfather. A third daughter was the wife of the late Mr W.E. Hall, the eminent writer on international law, and died without issue, and the fourth married Mr Reginald Somerled Macdonald, a lineal descendant of Flora Macdonald. She died leaving two daughters, one of whom was married to captain Duff Baker, R.A. and the other is the wife of Mr Hubert Crackanthorope, the author, son of Mr Montague Crackanthorpe."

Printed in the United Kingdom
by Lightning Source UK Ltd.
123232UK00002B/52-147/A